LONG DAY'S

JOURNEY

INTO NIGHT

Eugene O'Neill

LONG DAY'S JOURNEY INTO NIGHT

New Haven & London

Yale University Press

For Carlotta, on our 12th Wedding Anniversary

*Dearest: I give you the original script of this play
of old sorrow, written in tears and blood. A sadly
inappropriate gift, it would seem, for a day
celebrating happiness. But you will understand. I
mean it as a tribute to your love and tenderness which
gave me the faith in love that enabled me to
face my dead at last and write this play—write it
with deep pity and understanding and forgiveness for
all the four haunted Tyrones.*

*These twelve years, Beloved One, have been a
Journey into Light—into love. You know my gratitude.
And my love!*

GENE

*Tao House
July 22, 1941.*

Characters

JAMES TYRONE

MARY CAVAN TYRONE, *his wife*

JAMES TYRONE, JR., *their elder son*

EDMUND TYRONE, *their younger son*

CATHLEEN, *second girl*

Scenes

Act One

SCENE *Living room of James Tyrone's summer home on a morning in August, 1912.*

At rear are two double doorways with portieres. The one at right leads into a front parlor with the formally arranged, set appearance of a room rarely occupied. The other opens on a dark, windowless back parlor, never used except as a passage from living room to dining room. Against the wall between the doorways is a small bookcase, with a picture of Shakespeare above it, containing novels by Balzac, Zola, Stendhal, philosophical and sociological works by Schopenhauer, Nietzsche, Marx, Engels, Kropotkin, Max Stirner, plays by Ibsen, Shaw, Strindberg, poetry by Swinburne, Rossetti, Wilde, Ernest Dowson, Kipling, etc.

In the right wall, rear, is a screen door leading out on the porch which extends halfway around the house. Farther forward, a series of three windows looks over the front lawn to the harbor and the avenue that runs along the water front. A small wicker table and an ordinary oak desk are against the wall, flanking the windows.

In the left wall, a similar series of windows looks out on the grounds in back of the house. Beneath them is a wicker couch with cushions, its head toward rear. Farther back is a large, glassed-in bookcase with sets of Dumas, Victor Hugo, Charles Lever, three sets of Shakespeare, The World's Best Literature in fifty large volumes, Hume's History of England, Thiers' History of the Consulate and Empire, Smollett's History of England, Gibbon's Roman Empire and miscellaneous volumes of old plays, poetry, and several histories of Ireland. The astonishing thing about these sets is that all the volumes have the look of having been read and reread.

The hardwood floor is nearly covered by a rug, inoffensive in design and color. At center is a round table with a green shaded reading lamp, the cord plugged in one of the four sockets in the chandelier above. Around the table within reading-light range are four chairs, three of them wicker arm-chairs, the fourth (at right front of table) a varnished oak rocker with leather bottom.

It is around 8.30. Sunshine comes through the windows at right.

As the curtain rises, the family have just finished breakfast. MARY TYRONE and her husband enter together from the back parlor, coming from the dining room.

Mary is fifty-four, about medium height. She still has a young, graceful figure, a trifle plump, but showing little evidence of middle-aged waist and hips, although she is not tightly corseted. Her face is distinctly Irish in type. It must once have been extremely pretty, and is still striking. It does not match her healthy figure but is thin and pale with the bone structure prominent. Her nose is long and straight, her mouth wide with full, sensitive lips. She uses no rouge or any sort of make-up. Her high forehead is framed by thick, pure white hair. Accentuated by her pallor and white hair, her dark brown eyes appear black. They are unusually large and beautiful, with black brows and long curling lashes.

What strikes one immediately is her extreme nervousness. Her hands are never still. They were once beautiful hands, with long, tapering fingers, but rheumatism has knotted the joints and warped the fingers, so that now they have an ugly crippled look. One avoids looking at them, the more so be-cause one is conscious she is sensitive about their appearance and humiliated by her inability to control the nervousness which draws attention to them.

She is dressed simply but with a sure sense of what becomes

her. Her hair is arranged with fastidious care. Her voice is soft and attractive. When she is merry, there is a touch of Irish lilt in it.

Her most appealing quality is the simple, unaffected charm of a shy convent-girl youthfulness she has never lost—an innate unworldly innocence.

JAMES TYRONE is sixty-five but looks ten years younger. About five feet eight, broad-shouldered and deep-chested, he seems taller and slenderer because of his bearing, which has a soldierly quality of head up, chest out, stomach in, shoulders squared. His face has begun to break down but he is still remarkably good looking—a big, finely shaped head, a handsome profile, deep-set light-brown eyes. His grey hair is thin with a bald spot like a monk's tonsure.

The stamp of his profession is unmistakably on him. Not that he indulges in any of the deliberate temperamental posturings of the stage star. He is by nature and preference a simple, unpretentious man, whose inclinations are still close to his humble beginnings and his Irish farmer forebears. But the actor shows in all his unconscious habits of speech, movement and gesture. These have the quality of belonging to a studied technique. His voice is remarkably fine, resonant and flexible, and he takes great pride in it.

His clothes, assuredly, do not costume any romantic part. He wears a threadbare, ready-made, grey sack suit and shineless black shoes, a collar-less shirt with a thick white handkerchief knotted loosely around his throat. There is nothing picturesquely careless about this get-up. It is commonplace shabby. He believes in wearing his clothes to the limit of usefulness, is dressed now for gardening, and doesn't give a damn how he looks.

He has never been really sick a day in his life. He has no nerves. There is a lot of stolid, earthy peasant in him, mixed

*with streaks of sentimental melancholy and rare flashes of
intuitive sensibility.*

*Tyrone's arm is around his wife's waist as they appear from
the back parlor. Entering the living room he gives her a
playful hug.*

TYRONE

You're a fine armful now, Mary, with those twenty pounds you've
gained.

MARY
Smiles affectionately.
I've gotten too fat, you mean, dear. I really ought to reduce.

TYRONE

None of that, my lady! You're just right. We'll have no talk of re-
ducing. Is that why you ate so little breakfast?

MARY

So little? I thought I ate a lot.

TYRONE

You didn't. Not as much as I'd like to see, anyway.

MARY
Teasingly.
Oh you! You expect everyone to eat the enormous breakfast you do.
No one else in the world could without dying of indigestion.
She comes forward to stand by the right of table.

TYRONE
Following her.
I hope I'm not as big a glutton as that sounds.
With hearty satisfaction.
But thank God, I've kept my appetite and I've the digestion of a
young man of twenty, if I am sixty-five.

MARY

You surely have, James. No one could deny that.
*She laughs and sits in the wicker armchair at right rear of
table. He comes around in back of her and selects a cigar*

*from a box on the table and cuts off the end with a little
clipper. From the dining room Jamie's and Edmund's voices
are heard. Mary turns her head that way.*

Why did the boys stay in the dining room, I wonder? Cathleen must
be waiting to clear the table.

TYRONE
Jokingly but with an undercurrent of resentment.

It's a secret confab they don't want me to hear, I suppose. I'll bet
they're cooking up some new scheme to touch the Old Man.

*She is silent on this, keeping her head turned toward their
voices. Her hands appear on the table top, moving restlessly. He lights his cigar and sits down in the rocker at
right of table, which is his chair, and puffs contentedly.*

There's nothing like the first after-breakfast cigar, if it's a good one,
and this new lot have the right mellow flavor. They're a great bargain, too. I got them dead cheap. It was McGuire put me on to them.

MARY
A trifle acidly.

I hope he didn't put you on to any new piece of property at the same
time. His real estate bargains don't work out so well.

TYRONE
Defensively.

I wouldn't say that, Mary. After all, he was the one who advised me
to buy that place on Chestnut Street and I made a quick turnover on
it for a fine profit.

MARY
Smiles now with teasing affection.

I know. The famous one stroke of good luck. I'm sure McGuire
never dreamed—

Then she pats his hand.

Never mind, James. I know it's a waste of breath trying to convince
you you're not a cunning real estate speculator.

TYRONE
Huffily.

I've no such idea. But land is land, and it's safer than the stocks and
bonds of Wall Street swindlers.

15

Then placatingly.
But let's not argue about business this early in the morning.
> *A pause. The boys' voices are again heard and one of them has a fit of coughing. Mary listens worriedly. Her fingers play nervously on the table top.*

MARY

James, it's Edmund you ought to scold for not eating enough. He hardly touched anything except coffee. He needs to eat to keep up his strength. I keep telling him that but he says he simply has no appetite. Of course, there's nothing takes away your appetite like a bad summer cold.

TYRONE

Yes, it's only natural. So don't let yourself get worried—

MARY
> *Quickly.*
Oh, I'm not. I know he'll be all right in a few days if he takes care of himself.
> *As if she wanted to dismiss the subject but can't.*
But it does seem a shame he should have to be sick right now.

TYRONE

Yes, it is bad luck.
> *He gives her a quick, worried look.*
But you mustn't let it upset you, Mary. Remember, you've got to take care of yourself, too.

MARY
> *Quickly.*
I'm not upset. There's nothing to be upset about. What makes you think I'm upset?

TYRONE

Why, nothing, except you've seemed a bit high-strung the past few days.

MARY
> *Forcing a smile.*
I have? Nonsense, dear. It's your imagination.
> *With sudden tenseness.*

You really must not watch me all the time, James. I mean, it makes me self-conscious.

> TYRONE
> *Putting a hand over one of her nervously playing ones.*

Now, now, Mary. That's your imagination. If I've watched you it was to admire how fat and beautiful you looked.

> *His voice is suddenly moved by deep feeling.*

I can't tell you the deep happiness it gives me, darling, to see you as you've been since you came back to us, your dear old self again.

> *He leans over and kisses her cheek impulsively—then turning back adds with a constrained air.*

So keep up the good work, Mary.

> MARY
> *Has turned her head away.*

I will, dear.

> *She gets up restlessly and goes to the windows at right.*

Thank heavens, the fog is gone.

> *She turns back.*

I do feel out of sorts this morning. I wasn't able to get much sleep with that awful foghorn going all night long.

> TYRONE

Yes, it's like having a sick whale in the back yard. It kept me awake, too.

> MARY
> *Affectionately amused.*

Did it? You had a strange way of showing your restlessness. You were snoring so hard I couldn't tell which was the foghorn!

> *She comes to him, laughing, and pats his cheek playfully.*

Ten foghorns couldn't disturb you. You haven't a nerve in you. You've never had.

> TYRONE
> *His vanity piqued—testily.*

Nonsense. You always exaggerate about my snoring.

> MARY

I couldn't. If you could only hear yourself once—

17

A burst of laughter comes from the dining room. She turns her head, smiling.

What's the joke, I wonder?

TYRONE
Grumpily.

It's on me. I'll bet that much. It's always on the Old Man.

MARY
Teasingly.

Yes, it's terrible the way we all pick on you, isn't it? You're so abused!

She laughs—then with a pleased, relieved air.

Well, no matter what the joke is about, it's a relief to hear Edmund laugh. He's been so down in the mouth lately.

TYRONE
Ignoring this—resentfully.

Some joke of Jamie's, I'll wager. He's forever making sneering fun of somebody, that one.

MARY

Now don't start in on poor Jamie, dear.

Without conviction.

He'll turn out all right in the end, you wait and see.

TYRONE

He'd better start soon, then. He's nearly thirty-four.

MARY
Ignoring this.

Good heavens, are they going to stay in the dining room all day?

She goes to the back parlor doorway and calls.

Jamie! Edmund! Come in the living room and give Cathleen a chance to clear the table.

Edmund calls back, "We're coming, Mama." She goes back to the table.

TYRONE
Grumbling.

You'd find excuses for him no matter what he did.

MARY
Sitting down beside him, pats his hand.

Shush.

Their sons JAMES, JR., *and* EDMUND *enter together from the back parlor. They are both grinning, still chuckling over what had caused their laughter, and as they come forward they glance at their father and their grins grow broader.*

Jamie, the elder, is thirty-three. He has his father's broad-shouldered, deep-chested physique, is an inch taller and weighs less, but appears shorter and stouter because he lacks Tyrone's bearing and graceful carriage. He also lacks his father's vitality. The signs of premature disintegration are on him. His face is still good looking, despite marks of dissipation, but it has never been handsome like Tyrone's, although Jamie resembles him rather than his mother. He has fine brown eyes, their color midway between his father's lighter and his mother's darker ones. His hair is thinning and already there is indication of a bald spot like Tyrone's. His nose is unlike that of any other member of the family, pronouncedly aquiline. Combined with his habitual expression of cynicism it gives his countenance a Mephistophelian cast. But on the rare occasions when he smiles without sneering, his personality possesses the remnant of a humorous, romantic, irresponsible Irish charm—that of the beguiling ne'er-do-well, with a strain of the sentimentally poetic, attractive to women and popular with men.

He is dressed in an old sack suit, not as shabby as Tyrone's, and wears a collar and tie. His fair skin is sunburned a reddish, freckled tan.

Edmund is ten years younger than his brother, a couple of inches taller, thin and wiry. Where Jamie takes after his father, with little resemblance to his mother, Edmund looks like both his parents, but is more like his mother. Her big, dark eyes are the dominant feature in his long, narrow Irish face. His mouth has the same quality of hypersensitiveness hers possesses. His high forehead is hers accentuated, with dark brown hair, sunbleached to red at the ends, brushed straight back from it. But his nose is his father's and his face in profile recalls Tyrone's. Edmund's hands are noticeably like his mother's, with the same exceptionally long fingers. They even have to a minor degree the same nervousness. It is in the quality of extreme nervous sensibility that the likeness of Edmund to his mother is most marked.

He is plainly in bad health. Much thinner than he should be, his eyes appear feverish and his cheeks are sunken. His skin, in spite of being sunburned a deep brown, has a parched sallowness. He wears a shirt, collar and tie, no coat, old flannel trousers, brown sneakers.

MARY
Turns smilingly to them, in a merry tone that is a bit forced.
I've been teasing your father about his snoring.
To Tyrone.
I'll leave it to the boys, James. They must have heard you. No, not you, Jamie. I could hear you down the hall almost as bad as your father. You're like him. As soon as your head touches the pillow you're off and ten foghorns couldn't wake you.
She stops abruptly, catching Jamie's eyes regarding her with an uneasy, probing look. Her smile vanishes and her manner becomes self-conscious.
Why are you staring, Jamie?
Her hands flutter up to her hair.
Is my hair coming down? It's hard for me to do it up properly now. My eyes are getting so bad and I never can find my glasses.

JAMIE
Looks away guiltily.
Your hair's all right, Mama. I was only thinking how well you look.

TYRONE
Heartily.
Just what I've been telling her, Jamie. She's so fat and sassy, there'll soon be no holding her.

EDMUND

Yes, you certainly look grand, Mama.

> *She is reassured and smiles at him lovingly. He winks with a kidding grin.*

I'll back you up about Papa's snoring. Gosh, what a racket!

JAMIE

I heard him, too.

> *He quotes, putting on a ham-actor manner.*

"The Moor, I know his trumpet."

> *His mother and brother laugh.*

TYRONE

> *Scathingly.*

If it takes my snoring to make you remember Shakespeare instead of the dope sheet on the ponies, I hope I'll keep on with it.

MARY

Now, James! You mustn't be so touchy.

> *Jamie shrugs his shoulders and sits down in the chair on her right.*

EDMUND

> *Irritably.*

Yes, for Pete's sake, Papa! The first thing after breakfast! Give it a rest, can't you?

> *He slumps down in the chair at left of table next to his brother. His father ignores him.*

MARY

> *Reprovingly.*

Your father wasn't finding fault with you. You don't have to always take Jamie's part. You'd think you were the one ten years older.

JAMIE

> *Boredly.*

What's all the fuss about? Let's forget it.

TYRONE

> *Contemptuously.*

Yes, forget! Forget everything and face nothing! It's a convenient philosophy if you've no ambition in life except to—

MARY

She puts an arm around his shoulder—coaxingly.

James, do be quiet.

You must have gotten out of the wrong side of the bed this morning.

To the boys, changing the subject.

What were you two grinning about like Cheshire cats when you came in? What was the joke?

TYRONE

With a painful effort to be a good sport.

Yes, let us in on it, lads. I told your mother I knew damned well it would be one on me, but never mind that, I'm used to it.

JAMIE

Dryly.

Don't look at me. This is the Kid's story.

EDMUND

Grins.

I meant to tell you last night, Papa, and forgot it. Yesterday when I went for a walk I dropped in at the Inn—

MARY

Worriedly.

You shouldn't drink now, Edmund.

EDMUND

Ignoring this.

And who do you think I met there, with a beautiful bun on, but Shaughnessy, the tenant on that farm of yours.

MARY

Smiling.

That dreadful man! But he is funny.

TYRONE

Scowling.

He's not so funny when you're his landlord. He's a wily Shanty Mick, that one. He could hide behind a corkscrew. What's he complaining about now, Edmund—for I'm damned sure he's complaining. I suppose he wants his rent lowered. I let him have the place for almost nothing, just to keep someone on it, and he never pays that till I threaten to evict him.

EDMUND

No, he didn't beef about anything. He was so pleased with life he even bought a drink, and that's practically unheard of. He was delighted because he'd had a fight with your friend, Harker, the Standard Oil millionaire, and won a glorious victory.

MARY
With amused dismay.

Oh, Lord! James, you'll really have to do something—

TYRONE

Bad luck to Shaughnessy, anyway!

JAMIE
Maliciously.

I'll bet the next time you see Harker at the Club and give him the old respectful bow, he won't see you.

EDMUND

Yes. Harker will think you're no gentleman for harboring a tenant who isn't humble in the presence of a king of America.

TYRONE

Never mind the Socialist gabble. I don't care to listen—

MARY
Tactfully.

Go on with your story, Edmund.

EDMUND
Grins at his father provocatively.

Well, you remember, Papa, the ice pond on Harker's estate is right next to the farm, and you remember Shaughnessy keeps pigs. Well, it seems there's a break in the fence and the pigs have been bathing in the millionaire's ice pond, and Harker's foreman told him he was sure Shaughnessy had broken the fence on purpose to give his pigs a free wallow.

MARY
Shocked and amused.

Good heavens!

TYRONE
Sourly, but with a trace of admiration.
I'm sure he did, too, the dirty scallywag. It's like him.

EDMUND
So Harker came in person to rebuke Shaughnessy.
He chuckles.
A very bonehead play! If I needed any further proof that our ruling
plutocrats, especially the ones who inherited their boodle, are not
mental giants, that would clinch it.

TYRONE
With appreciation, before he thinks.
Yes, he'd be no match for Shaughnessy.
Then he growls.
Keep your damned anarchist remarks to yourself. I won't have them
in my house.
But he is full of eager anticipation.
What happened?

EDMUND
Harker had as much chance as I would with Jack Johnson. Shaughnessy got a few drinks under his belt and was waiting at the gate to
welcome him. He told me he never gave Harker a chance to open
his mouth. He began by shouting that he was no slave Standard Oil
could trample on. He was a King of Ireland, if he had his rights, and
scum was scum to him, no matter how much money it had stolen
from the poor.

MARY
Oh, Lord!
But she can't help laughing.

EDMUND
Then he accused Harker of making his foreman break down the fence
to entice the pigs into the ice pond in order to destroy them. The
poor pigs, Shaughnessy yelled, had caught their death of cold. Many
of them were dying of pneumonia, and several others had been taken
down with cholera from drinking the poisoned water. He told
Harker he was hiring a lawyer to sue him for damages. And he wound
up by saying that he had to put up with poison ivy, ticks, potato bugs,

snakes and skunks on his farm, but he was an honest man who drew the line somewhere, and he'd be damned if he'd stand for a Standard Oil thief trespassing. So would Harker kindly remove his dirty feet from the premises before he sicked the dog on him. And Harker did!

He and Jamie laugh.

MARY
Shocked but giggling.
Heavens, what a terrible tongue that man has!

TYRONE
Admiringly before he thinks.
The damned old scoundrel! By God, you can't beat him!
He laughs—then stops abruptly and scowls.
The dirty blackguard! He'll get me in serious trouble yet. I hope you told him I'd be mad as hell—

EDMUND
I told him you'd be tickled to death over the great Irish victory, and so you are. Stop faking, Papa.

TYRONE
Well, I'm not tickled to death.

MARY
Teasingly.
You are, too, James. You're simply delighted!

TYRONE
No, Mary, a joke is a joke, but—

EDMUND
I told Shaughnessy he should have reminded Harker that a Standard Oil millionaire ought to welcome the flavor of hog in his ice water as an appropriate touch.

TYRONE
The devil you did!
Frowning.
Keep your damned Socialist anarchist sentiments out of my affairs!

EDMUND
Shaughnessy almost wept because he hadn't thought of that one, but

he said he'd include it in a letter he's writing to Harker, along with a few other insults he'd overlooked.

He and Jamie laugh.

TYRONE

What are you laughing at? There's nothing funny—A fine son you are to help that blackguard get me into a lawsuit!

MARY

Now, James, don't lose your temper.

TYRONE

Turns on Jamie.

And you're worse than he is, encouraging him. I suppose you're regretting you weren't there to prompt Shaughnessy with a few nastier insults. You've a fine talent for that, if for nothing else.

MARY

James! There's no reason to scold Jamie.

Jamie is about to make some sneering remark to his father, but he shrugs his shoulders.

EDMUND

With sudden nervous exasperation.

Oh, for God's sake, Papa! If you're starting that stuff again, I'll beat it.

He jumps up.

I left my book upstairs, anyway.

He goes to the front parlor, saying disgustedly,

God, Papa, I should think you'd get sick of hearing yourself—

He disappears. Tyrone looks after him angrily.

MARY

You mustn't mind Edmund, James. Remember he isn't well.

Edmund can be heard coughing as he goes upstairs.

She adds nervously.

A summer cold makes anyone irritable.

JAMIE

Genuinely concerned.

It's not just a cold he's got. The Kid is damned sick.

*His father gives him a sharp warning look but he doesn't
see it.*

MARY
Turns on him resentfully.
Why do you say that? It *is* just a cold! Anyone can tell that! You
always imagine things!

TYRONE
With another warning glance at Jamie—easily.
All Jamie meant was Edmund might have a touch of something else,
too, which makes his cold worse.

JAMIE
Sure, Mama. That's all I meant.

TYRONE
Doctor Hardy thinks it might be a bit of malarial fever he caught
when he was in the tropics. If it is, quinine will soon cure it.

MARY
A look of contemptuous hostility flashes across her face.
Doctor Hardy! I wouldn't believe a thing he said, if he swore on a
stack of Bibles! I know what doctors are. They're all alike. Anything, they don't care what, to keep you coming to them.
*She stops short, overcome by a fit of acute self-consciousness
as she catches their eyes fixed on her. Her hands jerk nervously to her hair. She forces a smile.*
What is it? What are you looking at? Is my hair—?

TYRONE
*Puts his arm around her—with guilty heartiness, giving her
a playful hug.*
There's nothing wrong with your hair. The healthier and fatter you
get, the vainer you become. You'll soon spend half the day primping
before the mirror.

MARY
Half reassured.
I really should have new glasses. My eyes are so bad now.

TYRONE
With Irish blarney.

Your eyes are beautiful, and well you know it.
*He gives her a kiss. Her face lights up with a charming, shy
embarrassment. Suddenly and startlingly one sees in her face
the girl she had once been, not a ghost of the dead, but still
a living part of her.*

MARY
You mustn't be so silly, James. Right in front of Jamie!

TYRONE
Oh, he's on to you, too. He knows this fuss about eyes and hair is
only fishing for compliments. Eh, Jamie?

JAMIE
*His face has cleared, too, and there is an old boyish charm in
his loving smile at his mother.*
Yes. You can't kid us, Mama.

MARY
Laughs and an Irish lilt comes into her voice.
Go along with both of you!
Then she speaks with a girlish gravity.
But I did truly have beautiful hair once, didn't I, James?

TYRONE
The most beautiful in the world!

MARY
It was a rare shade of reddish brown and so long it came down below
my knees. You ought to remember it, too, Jamie. It wasn't until
after Edmund was born that I had a single grey hair. Then it began
to turn white.
The girlishness fades from her face.

TYRONE
Quickly.
And that made it prettier than ever.

MARY
Again embarrassed and pleased.

28

Will you listen to your father, Jamie—after thirty-five years of marriage! He isn't a great actor for nothing, is he? What's come over you, James? Are you pouring coals of fire on my head for teasing you about snoring? Well then, I take it all back. It must have been only the foghorn I heard.

She laughs, and they laugh with her. Then she changes to a brisk businesslike air.

But I can't stay with you any longer, even to hear compliments. I must see the cook about dinner and the day's marketing.

She gets up and sighs with humorous exaggeration.

Bridget is so lazy. And so sly. She begins telling me about her relatives so I can't get a word in edgeways and scold her. Well, I might as well get it over.

She goes to the back-parlor doorway, then turns, her face worried again.

You mustn't make Edmund work on the grounds with you, James, remember.

Again with the strange obstinate set to her face.

Not that he isn't strong enough, but he'd perspire and he might catch more cold.

She disappears through the back parlor. Tyrone turns on Jamie condemningly.

TYRONE

You're a fine lunkhead! Haven't you any sense? The one thing to avoid is saying anything that would get her more upset over Edmund.

JAMIE

Shrugging his shoulders.

All right. Have it your way. I think it's the wrong idea to let Mama go on kidding herself. It will only make the shock worse when she has to face it. Anyway, you can see she's deliberately fooling herself with that summer cold talk. She knows better.

TYRONE

Knows? Nobody knows yet.

JAMIE

Well, I do. I was with Edmund when he went to Doc Hardy on Monday. I heard him pull that touch of malaria stuff. He was stalling.

29

That isn't what he thinks any more. You know it as well as I do. You talked to him when you went uptown yesterday, didn't you?

TYRONE

He couldn't say anything for sure yet. He's to phone me today before Edmund goes to him.

JAMIE
Slowly.

He thinks it's consumption, doesn't he, Papa?

TYRONE
Reluctantly.

He said it might be.

JAMIE
Moved, his love for his brother coming out.

Poor kid! God damn it!
He turns on his father accusingly.
It might never have happened if you'd sent him to a real doctor when he first got sick.

TYRONE

What's the matter with Hardy? He's always been our doctor up here.

JAMIE

Everything's the matter with him! Even in this hick burg he's rated third class! He's a cheap old quack!

TYRONE

That's right! Run him down! Run down everybody! Everyone is a fake to you!

JAMIE
Contemptuously.

Hardy only charges a dollar. That's what makes you think he's a fine doctor!

TYRONE
Stung.

That's enough! You're not drunk now! There's no excuse—
He controls himself—a bit defensively.

If you mean I can't afford one of the fine society doctors who prey on the rich summer people—

JAMIE

Can't afford? You're one of the biggest property owners around here.

TYRONE

That doesn't mean I'm rich. It's all mortgaged—

JAMIE

Because you always buy more instead of paying off mortgages. If Edmund was a lousy acre of land you wanted, the sky would be the limit!

TYRONE

That's a lie! And your sneers against Doctor Hardy are lies! He doesn't put on frills, or have an office in a fashionable location, or drive around in an expensive automobile. That's what you pay for with those other five-dollars-to-look-at-your-tongue fellows, not their skill.

JAMIE

With a scornful shrug of his shoulders.

Oh, all right. I'm a fool to argue. You can't change the leopard's spots.

TYRONE

With rising anger.

No, you can't. You've taught me that lesson only too well. I've lost all hope you will ever change yours. You dare tell me what I can afford? You've never known the value of a dollar and never will! You've never saved a dollar in your life! At the end of each season you're penniless! You've thrown your salary away every week on whores and whiskey!

JAMIE

My salary! Christ!

TYRONE

It's more than you're worth, and you couldn't get that if it wasn't for me. If you weren't my son, there isn't a manager in the business who would give you a part, your reputation stinks so. As it is, I have to humble my pride and beg for you, saying you've turned over a new leaf, although I know it's a lie!

JAMIE

I never wanted to be an actor. You forced me on the stage.

TYRONE

That's a lie! You made no effort to find anything else to do. You left it to me to get you a job and I have no influence except in the theater. Forced you! You never wanted to do anything except loaf in barrooms! You'd have been content to sit back like a lazy lunk and sponge on me for the rest of your life! After all the money I'd wasted on your education, and all you did was get fired in disgrace from every college you went to!

JAMIE

Oh, for God's sake, don't drag up that ancient history!

TYRONE

It's not ancient history that you have to come home every summer to live on me.

JAMIE

I earn my board and lodging working on the grounds. It saves you hiring a man.

TYRONE

Bah! You have to be driven to do even that much!
His anger ebbs into a weary complaint.
I wouldn't give a damn if you ever displayed the slightest sign of gratitude. The only thanks is to have you sneer at me for a dirty miser, sneer at my profession, sneer at every damned thing in the world—except yourself.

JAMIE
Wryly.
That's not true, Papa. You can't hear me talking to myself, that's all.

TYRONE
Stares at him puzzledly, then quotes mechanically.
"Ingratitude, the vilest weed that grows"!

JAMIE

I could see that line coming! God, how many thousand times—!
> *He stops, bored with their quarrel, and shrugs his shoulders.*

All right, Papa. I'm a bum. Anything you like, so long as it stops the argument.

TYRONE
> *With indignant appeal now.*

If you'd get ambition in your head instead of folly! You're young yet. You could still make your mark. You had the talent to become a fine actor! You have it still. You're my son—!

JAMIE
> *Boredly.*

Let's forget me. I'm not interested in the subject. Neither are you.
> *Tyrone gives up. Jamie goes on casually.*

What started us on this? Oh, Doc Hardy. When is he going to call you up about Edmund?

TYRONE

Around lunch time.
> *He pauses—then defensively.*

I couldn't have sent Edmund to a better doctor. Hardy's treated him whenever he was sick up here, since he was knee high. He knows his constitution as no other doctor could. It's not a question of my being miserly, as you'd like to make out.
> *Bitterly.*

And what could the finest specialist in America do for Edmund, after he's deliberately ruined his health by the mad life he's led ever since he was fired from college? Even before that when he was in prep school, he began dissipating and playing the Broadway sport to imitate you, when he's never had your constitution to stand it. You're a healthy hulk like me—or you were at his age—but he's always been a bundle of nerves like his mother. I've warned him for years his body couldn't stand it, but he wouldn't heed me, and now it's too late.

JAMIE
> *Sharply.*

What do you mean, too late? You talk as if you thought—

33

TYRONE
Guiltily explosive.

Don't be a damned fool! I meant nothing but what's plain to anyone! His health has broken down and he may be an invalid for a long time.

JAMIE
Stares at his father, ignoring his explanation.

I know it's an Irish peasant idea consumption is fatal. It probably is when you live in a hovel on a bog, but over here, with modern treatment—

TYRONE

Don't I know that! What are you gabbing about, anyway? And keep your dirty tongue off Ireland, with your sneers about peasants and bogs and hovels!
Accusingly.

The less you say about Edmund's sickness, the better for your conscience! You're more responsible than anyone!

JAMIE
Stung.

That's a lie! I won't stand for that, Papa!

TYRONE

It's the truth! You've been the worst influence for him. He grew up admiring you as a hero! A fine example you set him! If you ever gave him advice except in the ways of rottenness, I've never heard of it! You made him old before his time, pumping him full of what you consider worldly wisdom, when he was too young to see that your mind was so poisoned by your own failure in life, you wanted to believe every man was a knave with his soul for sale, and every woman who wasn't a whore was a fool!

JAMIE
With a defensive air of weary indifference again.

All right. I did put Edmund wise to things, but not until I saw he'd started to raise hell, and knew he'd laugh at me if I tried the good advice, older brother stuff. All I did was make a pal of him and be absolutely frank so he'd learn from my mistakes that—

He shrugs his shoulders—cynically.
Well, that if you can't be good you can at least be careful.
His father snorts contemptuously. Suddenly Jamie becomes really moved.
That's a rotten accusation, Papa. You know how much the Kid means to me, and how close we've always been—not like the usual brothers! I'd do anything for him.

TYRONE
Impressed—mollifyingly.
I know you may have thought it was for the best, Jamie. I didn't say you did it deliberately to harm him.

JAMIE
Besides it's damned rot! I'd like to see anyone influence Edmund more than he wants to be. His quietness fools people into thinking they can do what they like with him. But he's stubborn as hell inside and what he does is what he wants to do, and to hell with anyone else! What had I to do with all the crazy stunts he's pulled in the last few years—working his way all over the map as a sailor and all that stuff. I thought that was a damned fool idea, and I told him so. You can't imagine me getting fun out of being on the beach in South America, or living in filthy dives, drinking rotgut, can you? No, thanks! I'll stick to Broadway, and a room with a bath, and bars that serve bonded Bourbon.

TYRONE
You and Broadway! It's made you what you are!
With a touch of pride.
Whatever Edmund's done, he's had the guts to go off on his own, where he couldn't come whining to me the minute he was broke.

JAMIE
Stung into sneering jealousy.
He's always come home broke finally, hasn't he? And what did his going away get him? Look at him now!
He is suddenly shamefaced.
Christ! That's a lousy thing to say. I don't mean that.

TYRONE
Decides to ignore this.

He's been doing well on the paper. I was hoping he'd found the work he wants to do at last.

JAMIE
Sneering jealously again.
A hick town rag! Whatever bull they hand you, they tell me he's a pretty bum reporter. If he weren't your son—
Ashamed again.
No, that's not true! They're glad to have him, but it's the special stuff that gets him by. Some of the poems and parodies he's written are damned good.
Grudgingly again.
Not that they'd ever get him anywhere on the big time.
Hastily.
But he's certainly made a damned good start.

TYRONE
Yes. He's made a start. You used to talk about wanting to become a newspaper man but you were never willing to start at the bottom. You expected—

JAMIE
Oh, for Christ's sake, Papa! Can't you lay off me!

TYRONE
Stares at him—then looks away—after a pause.
It's damnable luck Edmund should be sick right now. It couldn't have come at a worse time for him.
He adds, unable to conceal an almost furtive uneasiness.
Or for your mother. It's damnable she should have this to upset her, just when she needs peace and freedom from worry. She's been so well in the two months since she came home.
His voice grows husky and trembles a little.
It's been heaven to me. This home has been a home again. But I needn't tell you, Jamie.
His son looks at him, for the first time with an understanding sympathy. It is as if suddenly a deep bond of common feeling existed between them in which their antagonisms could be forgotten.

36

JAMIE
Almost gently.
I've felt the same way, Papa.

TYRONE
Yes, this time you can see how strong and sure of herself she is. She's a different woman entirely from the other times. She has control of her nerves—or she had until Edmund got sick. Now you can feel her growing tense and frightened underneath. I wish to God we could keep the truth from her, but we can't if he has to be sent to a sanatorium. What makes it worse is her father died of consumption. She worshiped him and she's never forgotten. Yes, it will be hard for her. But she can do it! She has the will power now! We must help her, Jamie, in every way we can!

JAMIE
Moved.
Of course, Papa.
Hesitantly.
Outside of nerves, she seems perfectly all right this morning.

TYRONE
With hearty confidence now.
Never better. She's full of fun and mischief.
Suddenly he frowns at Jamie suspiciously.
Why do you say, seems? Why shouldn't she be all right? What the hell do you mean?

JAMIE
Don't start jumping down my throat! God, Papa, this ought to be one thing we can talk over frankly without a battle.

TYRONE
I'm sorry, Jamie.
Tensely.
But go on and tell me—

JAMIE
There's nothing to tell. I was all wrong. It's just that last night— Well, you know how it is, I can't forget the past. I can't help being suspicious. Any more than you can.

Bitterly.

That's the hell of it. And it makes it hell for Mama! She watches us watching her—

TYRONE
Sadly.

I know.

Tensely.

Well, what was it? Can't you speak out?

JAMIE

Nothing, I tell you. Just my damned foolishness. Around three o'clock this morning, I woke up and heard her moving around in the spare room. Then she went to the bathroom. I pretended to be asleep. She stopped in the hall to listen, as if she wanted to make sure I was.

TYRONE
With forced scorn.

For God's sake, is that all? She told me herself the foghorn kept her awake all night, and every night since Edmund's been sick she's been up and down, going to his room to see how he was.

JAMIE
Eagerly.

Yes, that's right, she did stop to listen outside his room.

Hesitantly again.

It was her being in the spare room that scared me. I couldn't help remembering that when she starts sleeping alone in there, it has always been a sign—

TYRONE

It isn't this time! It's easily explained. Where else could she go last night to get away from my snoring?

He gives way to a burst of resentful anger.

By God, how you can live with a mind that sees nothing but the worst motives behind everything is beyond me!

JAMIE
Stung.

Don't pull that! I've just said I was all wrong. Don't you suppose I'm as glad of that as you are!

TYRONE
Mollifyingly.

I'm sure you are, Jamie.

A pause. His expression becomes somber. He speaks slowly with a superstitious dread.

It would be like a curse she can't escape if worry over Edmund— It was in her long sickness after bringing him into the world that she first—

JAMIE

She didn't have anything to do with it!

TYRONE

I'm not blaming her.

JAMIE
Bitingly.

Then who are you blaming? Edmund, for being born?

TYRONE

You damned fool! No one was to blame.

JAMIE

The bastard of a doctor was! From what Mama's said, he was another cheap quack like Hardy! You wouldn't pay for a first-rate—

TYRONE

That's a lie!
Furiously.

So I'm to blame! That's what you're driving at, is it? You evil-minded loafer!

JAMIE
Warningly as he hears his mother in the dining room.

Ssh!

Tyrone gets hastily to his feet and goes to look out the windows at right. Jamie speaks with a complete change of tone.

Well, if we're going to cut the front hedge today, we'd better go to work.

Mary comes in from the back parlor. She gives a quick, suspicious glance from one to the other, her manner nervously self-conscious.

39

TYRONE
Turns from the window—with an actor's heartiness.
Yes, it's too fine a morning to waste indoors arguing. Take a look
out the window, Mary. There's no fog in the harbor. I'm sure the
spell of it we've had is over now.

MARY
Going to him.
I hope so, dear.
To Jamie, forcing a smile.
Did I actually hear you suggesting work on the front hedge, Jamie?
Wonders will never cease! You must want pocket money badly.

JAMIE
Kiddingly.
When don't I?
He winks at her, with a derisive glance at his father.
I expect a salary of at least one large iron man at the end of the week
—to carouse on!

MARY
*Does not respond to his humor—her hands fluttering over
the front of her dress.*
What were you two arguing about?

JAMIE
Shrugs his shoulders.
The same old stuff.

MARY
I heard you say something about a doctor, and your father accusing
you of being evil-minded.

JAMIE
Quickly.
Oh, that. I was saying again Doc Hardy isn't my idea of the world's
greatest physician.

MARY
Knows he is lying—vaguely.
Oh. No, I wouldn't say he was, either.
Changing the subject—forcing a smile.

That Bridget! I thought I'd never get away. She told me all about her second cousin on the police force in St. Louis.

> *Then with nervous irritation.*

Well, if you're going to work on the hedge why don't you go?

> *Hastily.*

I mean, take advantage of the sunshine before the fog comes back.

> *Strangely, as if talking aloud to herself.*

Because I know it will.

> *Suddenly she is self-consciously aware that they are both staring fixedly at her—flurriedly, raising her hands.*

Or I should say, the rheumatism in my hands knows. It's a better weather prophet than you are, James.

> *She stares at her hands with fascinated repulsion.*

Ugh! How ugly they are! Who'd ever believe they were once beautiful?

> *They stare at her with a growing dread.*

TYRONE

> *Takes her hands and gently pushes them down.*

Now, now, Mary. None of that foolishness. They're the sweetest hands in the world.

> *She smiles, her face lighting up, and kisses him gratefully. He turns to his son.*

Come on Jamie. Your mother's right to scold us. The way to start work is to start work. The hot sun will sweat some of that booze fat off your middle.

> *He opens the screen door and goes out on the porch and disappears down a flight of steps leading to the ground. Jamie rises from his chair and, taking off his coat, goes to the door. At the door he turns back but avoids looking at her, and she does not look at him.*

JAMIE

> *With an awkward, uneasy tenderness.*

We're all so proud of you, Mama, so darned happy.

> *She stiffens and stares at him with a frightened defiance. He flounders on.*

But you've still got to be careful. You mustn't worry so much about Edmund. He'll be all right.

41

MARY
With a stubborn, bitterly resentful look.
Of course, he'll be all right. And I don't know what you mean, warning me to be careful.

JAMIE
Rebuffed and hurt, shrugs his shoulders.
All right, Mama. I'm sorry I spoke.
He goes out on the porch. She waits rigidly until he disappears down the steps. Then she sinks down in the chair he had occupied, her face betraying a frightened, furtive desperation, her hands roving over the table top, aimlessly moving objects around. She hears Edmund descending the stairs in the front hall. As he nears the bottom he has a fit of coughing. She springs to her feet, as if she wanted to run away from the sound, and goes quickly to the windows at right. She is looking out, apparently calm, as he enters from the front parlor, a book in one hand. She turns to him, her lips set in a welcoming, motherly smile.

MARY
Here you are. I was just going upstairs to look for you.

EDMUND
I waited until they went out. I don't want to mix up in any arguments. I feel too rotten.

MARY
Almost resentfully.
Oh, I'm sure you don't feel half as badly as you make out. You're such a baby. You like to get us worried so we'll make a fuss over you.
Hastily.
I'm only teasing, dear. I know how miserably uncomfortable you must be. But you feel better today, don't you?
Worriedly, taking his arm.
All the same, you've grown much too thin. You need to rest all you can. Sit down and I'll make you comfortable.
He sits down in the rocking chair and she puts a pillow behind his back.
There. How's that?

42

EDMUND

Grand. Thanks, Mama.

MARY

Kisses him—tenderly.

All you need is your mother to nurse you. Big as you are, you're still the baby of the family to me, you know.

EDMUND

Takes her hand—with deep seriousness.

Never mind me. You take care of yourself. That's all that counts.

MARY

Evading his eyes.

But I am, dear.

Forcing a laugh.

Heavens, don't you see how fat I've grown! I'll have to have all my dresses let out.

She turns away and goes to the windows at right. She attempts a light, amused tone.

They've started clipping the hedge. Poor Jamie! How he hates working in front where everyone passing can see him. There go the Chatfields in their new Mercedes. It's a beautiful car, isn't it? Not like our secondhand Packard. Poor Jamie! He bent almost under the hedge so they wouldn't notice him. They bowed to your father and he bowed back as if he were taking a curtain call. In that filthy old suit I've tried to make him throw away.

Her voice has grown bitter.

Really, he ought to have more pride than to make such a show of himself.

EDMUND

He's right not to give a damn what anyone thinks. Jamie's a fool to care about the Chatfields. For Pete's sake, who ever heard of them outside this hick burg?

MARY

With satisfaction.

No one. You're quite right, Edmund. Big frogs in a small puddle. It is stupid of Jamie.

She pauses, looking out the window—then with an under-current of lonely yearning.

Still, the Chatfields and people like them stand for something. I mean they have decent, presentable homes they don't have to be ashamed of. They have friends who entertain them and whom they entertain. They're not cut off from everyone.

She turns back from the window.

Not that I want anything to do with them. I've always hated this town and everyone in it. You know that. I never wanted to live here in the first place, but your father liked it and insisted on building this house, and I've had to come here every summer.

EDMUND

Well, it's better than spending the summer in a New York hotel, isn't it? And this town's not so bad. I like it well enough. I suppose because it's the only home we've had.

MARY

I've never felt it was my home. It was wrong from the start. Everything was done in the cheapest way. Your father would never spend the money to make it right. It's just as well we haven't any friends here. I'd be ashamed to have them step in the door. But he's never wanted family friends. He hates calling on people, or receiving them. All he likes is to hobnob with men at the Club or in a barroom. Jamie and you are the same way, but you're not to blame. You've never had a chance to meet decent people here. I know you both would have been so different if you'd been able to associate with nice girls instead of— You'd never have disgraced yourselves as you have, so that now no respectable parents will let their daughters be seen with you.

EDMUND

Irritably.

Oh, Mama, forget it! Who cares? Jamie and I would be bored stiff. And about the Old Man, what's the use of talking? You can't change him.

MARY

Mechanically rebuking.

Don't call your father the Old Man. You should have more respect.

Then dully.

I know it's useless to talk. But sometimes I feel so lonely.

Her lips quiver and she keeps her head turned away.

EDMUND

Anyway, you've got to be fair, Mama. It may have been all his fault in the beginning, but you know that later on, even if he'd wanted to, we couldn't have had people here—

He flounders guiltily.

I mean, you wouldn't have wanted them.

MARY

Wincing—her lips quivering pitifully.

Don't. I can't bear having you remind me.

EDMUND

Don't take it that way! Please, Mama! I'm trying to help. Because it's bad for you to forget. The right way is to remember. So you'll always be on your guard. You know what's happened before.

Miserably.

God, Mama, you know I hate to remind you. I'm doing it because it's been so wonderful having you home the way you've been, and it would be terrible—

MARY

Strickenly.

Please, dear. I know you mean it for the best, but—

A defensive uneasiness comes into her voice again.

I don't understand why you should suddenly say such things. What put it in your mind this morning?

EDMUND

Evasively.

Nothing. Just because I feel rotten and blue, I suppose.

MARY

Tell me the truth. Why are you so suspicious all of a sudden?

EDMUND

I'm not!

MARY

Oh, yes you are. I can feel it. Your father and Jamie, too—particularly Jamie.

EDMUND

Now don't start imagining things, Mama.

MARY

Her hands fluttering.

It makes it so much harder, living in this atmosphere of constant suspicion, knowing everyone is spying on me, and none of you believe in me, or trust me.

EDMUND

That's crazy, Mama. We do trust you.

MARY

If there was only some place I could go to get away for a day, or even an afternoon, some woman friend I could talk to—not about anything serious, simply laugh and gossip and forget for a while—someone besides the servants—that stupid Cathleen!

EDMUND

Gets up worriedly and puts his arm around her.

Stop it, Mama. You're getting yourself worked up over nothing.

MARY

Your father goes out. He meets his friends in barrooms or at the Club. You and Jamie have the boys you know. You go out. But I am alone. I've always been alone.

EDMUND

Soothingly.

Come now! You know that's a fib. One of us always stays around to keep you company, or goes with you in the automobile when you take a drive.

MARY

Bitterly.

Because you're afraid to trust me alone!

She turns on him—sharply.

I insist you tell me why you act so differently this morning—why you felt you had to remind me—

EDMUND

Hesitates—then blurts out guiltily.

It's stupid. It's just that I wasn't asleep when you came in my room last night. You didn't go back to your and Papa's room. You went in the spare room for the rest of the night.

MARY

Because your father's snoring was driving me crazy! For heaven's sake, haven't I often used the spare room as my bedroom?
Bitterly.
But I see what you thought. That was when—

EDMUND

Too vehemently.
I didn't think anything!

MARY

So you pretended to be asleep in order to spy on me!

EDMUND

No! I did it because I knew if you found out I was feverish and couldn't sleep, it would upset you.

MARY

Jamie was pretending to be asleep, too, I'm sure, and I suppose your father—

EDMUND

Stop it, Mama!

MARY

Oh, I can't bear it, Edmund, when even you—!
Her hands flutter up to pat her hair in their aimless, dis-tracted way. Suddenly a strange undercurrent of revenge-fulness comes into her voice.
It would serve all of you right if it was true!

EDMUND

Mama! Don't say that! That's the way you talk when—

MARY

Stop suspecting me! Please, dear! You hurt me! I couldn't sleep be-cause I was thinking about you. That's the real reason! I've been so worried ever since you've been sick.

She puts her arms around him and hugs him with a frightened, protective tenderness.

EDMUND
Soothingly.

That's foolishness. You know it's only a bad cold.

MARY

Yes, of course, I know that!

EDMUND

But listen, Mama. I want you to promise me that even if it should turn out to be something worse, you'll know I'll soon be all right again, anyway, and you won't worry yourself sick, and you'll keep on taking care of yourself—

MARY
Frightenedly.

I won't listen when you're so silly! There's absolutely no reason to talk as if you expected something dreadful! Of course, I promise you. I give you my sacred word of honor!
Then with a sad bitterness.

But I suppose you're remembering I've promised before on my word of honor.

EDMUND

No!

MARY
Her bitterness receding into a resigned helplessness.

I'm not blaming you, dear. How can you help it? How can any one of us forget?
Strangely.

That's what makes it so hard—for all of us. We can't forget.

EDMUND
Grabs her shoulder.

Mama! Stop it!

MARY
Forcing a smile.

All right, dear. I didn't mean to be so gloomy. Don't mind me. Here.

Let me feel your head. Why, it's nice and cool. You certainly haven't any fever now.

EDMUND

Forget! It's you—

MARY

But I'm quite all right, dear.

With a quick, strange, calculating, almost sly glance at him.
Except I naturally feel tired and nervous this morning, after such a bad night. I really ought to go upstairs and lie down until lunch time and take a nap.

He gives her an instinctive look of suspicion—then, ashamed of himself, looks quickly away. She hurries on nervously.
What are you going to do? Read here? It would be much better for you to go out in the fresh air and sunshine. But don't get overheated, remember. Be sure and wear a hat.

She stops, looking straight at him now. He avoids her eyes. There is a tense pause. Then she speaks jeeringly.
Or are you afraid to trust me alone?

EDMUND

Tormentedly.

No! Can't you stop talking like that! I think you ought to take a nap.

He goes to the screen door—forcing a joking tone.
I'll go down and help Jamie bear up. I love to lie in the shade and watch him work.

He forces a laugh in which she makes herself join. Then he goes out on the porch and disappears down the steps. Her first reaction is one of relief. She appears to relax. She sinks down in one of the wicker armchairs at rear of table and leans her head back, closing her eyes. But suddenly she grows terribly tense again. Her eyes open and she strains forward, seized by a fit of nervous panic. She begins a desperate battle with herself. Her long fingers, warped and knotted by rheumatism, drum on the arms of the chair, driven by an insistent life of their own, without her consent.

CURTAIN

Act Two, Scene One

SCENE *The same. It is around quarter to one. No sunlight comes into the room now through the windows at right. Outside the day is still fine but increasingly sultry, with a faint haziness in the air which softens the glare of the sun.*

Edmund sits in the armchair at left of table, reading a book. Or rather he is trying to concentrate on it but cannot. He seems to be listening for some sound from upstairs. His manner is nervously apprehensive and he looks more sickly than in the previous act.

The second girl, CATHLEEN, *enters from the back parlor. She carries a tray on which is a bottle of bonded Bourbon, several whiskey glasses, and a pitcher of ice water. She is a buxom Irish peasant, in her early twenties, with a red-cheeked comely face, black hair and blue eyes—amiable, ignorant, clumsy, and possessed by a dense, well-meaning stupidity. She puts the tray on the table. Edmund pretends to be so absorbed in his book he does not notice her, but she ignores this.*

CATHLEEN
With garrulous familiarity.
Here's the whiskey. It'll be lunch time soon. Will I call your father and Mister Jamie, or will you?

EDMUND
Without looking up from his book.
You do it.

CATHLEEN
It's a wonder your father wouldn't look at his watch once in a while. He's a divil for making the meals late, and then Bridget curses me as if I was to blame. But he's a grand handsome man, if he is old. You'll never see the day you're as good looking—nor Mister Jamie, either.

She chuckles.

I'll wager Mister Jamie wouldn't miss the time to stop work and have his drop of whiskey if he had a watch to his name!

CATHLEEN
Gives up trying to ignore her and grins.

You win that one.

CATHLEEN

And here's another I'd win, that you're making me call them so you can sneak a drink before they come.

EDMUND

Well, I hadn't thought of that—

CATHLEEN

Oh no, not you! Butter wouldn't melt in your mouth, I suppose.

EDMUND

But now you suggest it—

CATHLEEN
Suddenly primly virtuous.

I'd never suggest a man or a woman touch drink, Mister Edmund. Sure, didn't it kill an uncle of mine in the old country.
Relenting.
Still, a drop now and then is no harm when you're in low spirits, or have a bad cold.

EDMUND

Thanks for handing me a good excuse.
Then with forced casualness.
You'd better call my mother, too.

CATHLEEN

What for? She's always on time without any calling. God bless her, she has some consideration for the help.

EDMUND

She's been taking a nap.

CATHLEEN

She wasn't asleep when I finished my work upstairs a while back.

She was lying down in the spare room with her eyes wide open. She'd a terrible headache, she said.

EDMUND
His casualness more forced.
Oh well then, just call my father.

CATHLEEN
Goes to the screen door, grumbling good-naturedly.
No wonder my feet kill me each night. I won't walk out in this heat and get sunstroke. I'll call from the porch.
She goes out on the side porch, letting the screen door slam behind her, and disappears on her way to the front porch. A moment later she is heard shouting.
Mister Tyrone! Mister Jamie! It's time!
Edmund, who has been staring frightenedly before him, forgetting his book, springs to his feet nervously.

EDMUND
God, what a wench!
He grabs the bottle and pours a drink, adds ice water and drinks. As he does so, he hears someone coming in the front door. He puts the glass hastily on the tray and sits down again, opening his book. Jamie comes in from the front parlor, his coat over his arm. He has taken off collar and tie and carries them in his hand. He is wiping sweat from his forehead with a handkerchief. Edmund looks up as if his reading was interrupted. Jamie takes one look at the bottle and glasses and smiles cynically.

JAMIE
Sneaking one, eh? Cut out the bluff, Kid. You're a rottener actor than I am.

EDMUND
Grins.
Yes, I grabbed one while the going was good.

JAMIE
Puts a hand affectionately on his shoulder.
That's better. Why kid me? We're pals, aren't we?

EDMUND

I wasn't sure it was you coming.

JAMIE

I made the Old Man look at his watch. I was halfway up the walk when Cathleen burst into song. Our wild Irish lark! She ought to be a train announcer.

EDMUND

That's what drove me to drink. Why don't you sneak one while you've got a chance?

JAMIE

I was thinking of that little thing.
He goes quickly to the window at right.
The Old Man was talking to old Captain Turner. Yes, he's still at it.
He comes back and takes a drink.
And now to cover up from his eagle eye. He memorizes the level in the bottle after every drink.
He measures two drinks of water and pours them in the whiskey bottle and shakes it up.
There. That fixes it.
He pours water in the glass and sets it on the table by Edmund.
And here's the water you've been drinking.

EDMUND

Fine! You don't think it will fool him, do you?

JAMIE

Maybe not, but he can't prove it.
Putting on his collar and tie.
I hope he doesn't forget lunch listening to himself talk. I'm hungry.
He sits across the table from Edmund—irritably.
That's what I hate about working down in front. He puts on an act for every damned fool that comes along.

EDMUND

Gloomily.
You're in luck to be hungry. The way I feel I don't care if I ever eat again.

JAMIE
Gives him a glance of concern.
Listen, Kid. You know me. I've never lectured you, but Doctor Hardy was right when he told you to cut out the redeye.

EDMUND
Oh, I'm going to after he hands me the bad news this afternoon. A few before then won't make any difference.

JAMIE
Hesitates—then slowly.
I'm glad you've got your mind prepared for bad news. It won't be such a jolt.
He catches Edmund staring at him.
I mean, it's a cinch you're really sick, and it would be wrong dope to kid yourself.

EDMUND
Disturbed.
I'm not. I know how rotten I feel, and the fever and chills I get at night are no joke. I think Doctor Hardy's last guess was right. It must be the damned malaria come back on me.

JAMIE
Maybe, but don't be too sure.

EDMUND
Why? What do you think it is?

JAMIE
Hell, how would I know? I'm no Doc.
Abruptly.
Where's Mama?

EDMUND
Upstairs.

JAMIE
Looks at him sharply.
When did she go up?

EDMUND
Oh, about the time I came down to the hedge, I guess. She said she was going to take a nap.

JAMIE

You didn't tell me—

EDMUND
Defensively.
Why should I? What about it? She was tired out. She didn't get much sleep last night.

JAMIE
I know she didn't.
A pause. The brothers avoid looking at each other.

EDMUND
That damned foghorn kept me awake, too.
Another pause.

JAMIE
She's been upstairs alone all morning, eh? You haven't seen her?

EDMUND
No. I've been reading here. I wanted to give her a chance to sleep.

JAMIE
Is she coming down to lunch?

EDMUND
Of course.

JAMIE
Dryly.
No of course about it. She might not want any lunch. Or she might start having most of her meals alone upstairs. That's happened, hasn't it?

EDMUND
With frightened resentment.
Cut it out, Jamie! Can't you think anything but—?
Persuasively.
You're all wrong to suspect anything. Cathleen saw her not long ago. Mama didn't tell her she wouldn't be down to lunch.

JAMIE
Then she wasn't taking a nap?

EDMUND

Not right then, but she was lying down, Cathleen said.

JAMIE

In the spare room?

EDMUND

Yes. For Pete's sake, what of it?

JAMIE
Bursts out.
You damned fool! Why did you leave her alone so long? Why didn't you stick around?

EDMUND

Because she accused me—and you and Papa—of spying on her all the time and not trusting her. She made me feel ashamed. I know how rotten it must be for her. And she promised on her sacred word of honor—

JAMIE
With a bitter weariness.
You ought to know that doesn't mean anything.

EDMUND

It does this time!

JAMIE

That's what we thought the other times.
He leans over the table to give his brother's arm an affection-ate grasp.
Listen, Kid, I know you think I'm a cynical bastard, but remember I've seen a lot more of this game than you have. You never knew what was really wrong until you were in prep school. Papa and I kept it from you. But I was wise ten years or more before we had to tell you. I know the game backwards and I've been thinking all morning of the way she acted last night when she thought we were asleep. I haven't been able to think of anything else. And now you tell me she got you to leave her alone upstairs all morning.

EDMUND

She didn't! You're crazy!

JAMIE
Placatingly.

All right, Kid. Don't start a battle with me. I hope as much as you do I'm crazy. I've been as happy as hell because I'd really begun to believe that this time—

He stops—looking through the front parlor toward the hall —lowering his voice, hurriedly.

She's coming downstairs. You win on that. I guess I'm a damned suspicious louse.

They grow tense with a hopeful, fearful expectancy. Jamie mutters.

Damn! I wish I'd grabbed another drink.

EDMUND

Me, too.

He coughs nervously and this brings on a real fit of coughing. Jamie glances at him with worried pity. Mary enters from the front parlor. At first one notices no change except that she appears to be less nervous, to be more as she was when we first saw her after breakfast, but then one becomes aware that her eyes are brighter, and there is a peculiar detachment in her voice and manner, as if she were a little withdrawn from her words and actions.

MARY

Goes worriedly to Edmund and puts her arm around him.

You mustn't cough like that. It's bad for your throat. You don't want to get a sore throat on top of your cold.

She kisses him. He stops coughing and gives her a quick apprehensive glance, but if his suspicions are aroused her tenderness makes him renounce them and he believes what he wants to believe for the moment. On the other hand, Jamie knows after one probing look at her that his suspicions are justified. His eyes fall to stare at the floor, his face sets in an expression of embittered, defensive cynicism. Mary goes on, half sitting on the arm of Edmund's chair, her arm around him, so her face is above and behind his and he cannot look into her eyes.

But I seem to be always picking on you, telling you don't do this and don't do that. Forgive me, dear. It's just that I want to take care of you.

EDMUND

I know, Mama. How about you? Do you feel rested?

MARY

Yes, ever so much better. I've been lying down ever since you went out. It's what I needed after such a restless night. I don't feel nervous now.

EDMUND

That's fine.

He pats her hand on his shoulder. Jamie gives him a strange, almost contemptuous glance, wondering if his brother can really mean this. Edmund does not notice but his mother does.

MARY

In a forced teasing tone.

Good heavens, how down in the mouth you look, Jamie. What's the matter now?

JAMIE

Without looking at her.

Nothing.

MARY

Oh, I'd forgotten you've been working on the front hedge. That accounts for your sinking into the dumps, doesn't it?

JAMIE

If you want to think so, Mama.

MARY

Keeping her tone.

Well, that's the effect it always has, isn't it? What a big baby you are! Isn't he, Edmund?

EDMUND

He's certainly a fool to care what anyone thinks.

MARY

Strangely.

Yes, the only way is to make yourself not care.

> *She catches Jamie giving her a bitter glance and changes the subject.*

Where is your father? I heard Cathleen call him.

EDMUND

Gabbing with old Captain Turner, Jamie says. He'll be late, as usual.

> *Jamie gets up and goes to the windows at right, glad of an excuse to turn his back.*

MARY

I've told Cathleen time and again she must go wherever he is and tell him. The idea of screaming as if this were a cheap boardinghouse!

JAMIE

> *Looking out the window.*

She's down there now.

> *Sneeringly.*

Interrupting the famous Beautiful Voice! She should have more respect.

MARY

> *Sharply—letting her resentment toward him come out.*

It's you who should have more respect! Stop sneering at your father! I won't have it! You ought to be proud you're his son! He may have his faults. Who hasn't? But he's worked hard all his life. He made his way up from ignorance and poverty to the top of his profession! Everyone else admires him and you should be the last one to sneer— you, who, thanks to him, have never had to work hard in your life!

> *Stung, Jamie has turned to stare at her with accusing antagonism. Her eyes waver guiltily and she adds in a tone which begins to placate.*

Remember your father is getting old, Jamie. You really ought to show more consideration.

JAMIE

I ought to?

EDMUND

> *Uneasily.*

Oh, dry up, Jamie!

Jamie looks out the window again.

And, for Pete's sake, Mama, why jump on Jamie all of a sudden?

MARY
Bitterly.

Because he's always sneering at someone else, always looking for the worst weakness in everyone.

Then with a strange, abrupt change to a detached, impersonal tone.

But I suppose life has made him like that, and he can't help it. None of us can help the things life has done to us. They're done before you realize it, and once they're done they make you do other things until at last everything comes between you and what you'd like to be, and you've lost your true self forever.

Edmund is made apprehensive by her strangeness. He tries to look up in her eyes but she keeps them averted. Jamie turns to her—then looks quickly out of the window again.

JAMIE
Dully.

I'm hungry. I wish the Old Man would get a move on. It's a rotten trick the way he keeps meals waiting, and then beefs because they're spoiled.

MARY
With a resentment that has a quality of being automatic and on the surface while inwardly she is indifferent.

Yes, it's very trying, Jamie. You don't know how trying. You don't have to keep house with summer servants who don't care because they know it isn't a permanent position. The really good servants are all with people who have homes and not merely summer places. And your father won't even pay the wages the best summer help ask. So every year I have stupid, lazy greenhorns to deal with. But you've heard me say this a thousand times. So has he, but it goes in one ear and out the other. He thinks money spent on a home is money wasted. He's lived too much in hotels. Never the best hotels, of course. Second-rate hotels. He doesn't understand a home. He doesn't feel at home in it. And yet, he wants a home. He's even proud of having this shabby place. He loves it here.

She laughs—a hopeless and yet amused laugh.
It's really funny, when you come to think of it. He's a peculiar man.

EDMUND
Again attempting uneasily to look up in her eyes.
What makes you ramble on like that, Mama?

MARY
Quickly casual—patting his cheek.
Why, nothing in particular, dear. It *is* foolish.
As she speaks, Cathleen enters from the back parlor.

CATHLEEN
Volubly.
Lunch is ready, Ma'am, I went down to Mister Tyrone, like you ordered, and he said he'd come right away, but he kept on talking to that man, telling him of the time when—

MARY
Indifferently.
All right, Cathleen. Tell Bridget I'm sorry but she'll have to wait a few minutes until Mister Tyrone is here.
Cathleen mutters, "Yes, Ma'am," and goes off through the back parlor, grumbling to herself.

JAMIE
Damn it! Why don't you go ahead without him? He's told us to.

MARY
With a remote, amused smile.
He doesn't mean it. Don't you know your father yet? He'd be so terribly hurt.

EDMUND
Jumps up—as if he was glad of an excuse to leave.
I'll make him get a move on.
He goes out on the side porch. A moment later he is heard calling from the porch exasperatedly.
Hey! Papa! Come on! We can't wait all day!
Mary has risen from the arm of the chair. Her hands play restlessly over the table top. She does not look at Jamie but

she feels the cynically appraising glance he gives her face and hands.

MARY
Tensely.
Why do you stare like that?

JAMIE
You know.
He turns back to the window.

MARY
I don't know.

JAMIE
Oh, for God's sake, do you think you can fool me, Mama? I'm not blind.

MARY
Looks directly at him now, her face set again in an expression of blank, stubborn denial.
I don't know what you're talking about.

JAMIE
No? Take a look at your eyes in the mirror!

EDMUND
Coming in from the porch.
I got Papa moving. He'll be here in a minute.
With a glance from one to the other, which his mother avoids—uneasily.
What's happened? What's the matter, Mama?

MARY
Disturbed by his coming, gives way to a flurry of guilty, nervous excitement.
Your brother ought to be ashamed of himself. He's been insinuating I don't know what.

EDMUND
Turns on Jamie.
God damn you!

*He takes a threatening step toward him. Jamie turns his back
with a shrug and looks out the window.*

MARY
More upset, grabs Edmund's arm—excitedly.

Stop this at once, do you hear me? How dare you use such language
before me!

*Abruptly her tone and manner change to the strange detach-
ment she has shown before.*

It's wrong to blame your brother. He can't help being what the past
has made him. Any more than your father can. Or you. Or I.

EDMUND
Frightenedly—with a desperate hoping against hope.

He's a liar! It's a lie, isn't it, Mama?

MARY
Keeping her eyes averted.

What is a lie? Now you're talking in riddles like Jamie.

*Then her eyes meet his stricken, accusing look. She stam-
mers.*

Edmund! Don't!

*She looks away and her manner instantly regains the quality
of strange detachment—calmly.*

There's your father coming up the steps now. I must tell Bridget.

*She goes through the back parlor. Edmund moves slowly to
his chair. He looks sick and hopeless.*

JAMIE
From the window, without looking around.

Well?

EDMUND
*Refusing to admit anything to his brother yet—weakly de-
fiant.*

Well, what? You're a liar.

*Jamie again shrugs his shoulders. The screen door on the
front porch is heard closing. Edmund says dully.*

Here's Papa. I hope he loosens up with the old bottle.

*Tyrone comes in through the front parlor. He is putting on
his coat.*

TYRONE

Sorry I'm late. Captain Turner stopped to talk and once he starts gabbing you can't get away from him.

JAMIE
Without turning—dryly.
You mean once he starts listening.
His father regards him with dislike. He comes to the table with a quick measuring look at the bottle of whiskey. Without turning, Jamie senses this.
It's all right. The level in the bottle hasn't changed.

TYRONE
I wasn't noticing that.
He adds caustically.
As if it proved anything with you around. I'm on to your tricks.

EDMUND
Dully.
Did I hear you say, let's all have a drink?

TYRONE
Frowns at him.
Jamie is welcome after his hard morning's work, but I won't invite you. Doctor Hardy—

EDMUND
To hell with Doctor Hardy! One isn't going to kill me. I feel—all in, Papa.

TYRONE
With a worried look at him—putting on a fake heartiness.
Come along, then. It's before a meal and I've always found that good whiskey, taken in moderation as an appetizer, is the best of tonics.
Edmund gets up as his father passes the bottle to him. He pours a big drink. Tyrone frowns admonishingly.
I said, in moderation.
He pours his own drink and passes the bottle to Jamie, grumbling.
It'd be a waste of breath mentioning moderation to you.
Ignoring the hint, Jamie pours a big drink. His father

scowls—then, giving it up, resumes his hearty air, raising his glass.

Well, here's health and happiness!

Edmund gives a bitter laugh.

EDMUND

That's a joke!

TYRONE

What is?

EDMUND

Nothing. Here's how.

They drink.

TYRONE

Becoming aware of the atmosphere.

What's the matter here? There's gloom in the air you could cut with a knife.

Turns on Jamie resentfully.

You got the drink you were after, didn't you? Why are you wearing that gloomy look on your mug?

JAMIE

Shrugging his shoulders.

You won't be singing a song yourself soon.

EDMUND

Shut up, Jamie.

TYRONE

Uneasy now—changing the subject.

I thought lunch was ready. I'm hungry as a hunter. Where is your mother?

MARY

Returning through the back parlor, calls.

Here I am.

She comes in. She is excited and self-conscious. As she talks, she glances everywhere except at any of their faces.

I've had to calm down Bridget. She's in a tantrum over your being late again, and I don't blame her. If your lunch is dried up from waiting in the oven, she said it served you right, you could like it or leave it for all she cared.

With increasing excitement.

Oh, I'm so sick and tired of pretending this is a home! You won't help me! You won't put yourself out the least bit! You don't know how to act in a home! You don't really want one! You never have wanted one—never since the day we were married! You should have remained a bachelor and lived in second-rate hotels and entertained your friends in barrooms!

She adds strangely, as if she were now talking aloud to herself rather than to Tyrone.

Then nothing would ever have happened.

They stare at her. Tyrone knows now. He suddenly looks a tired, bitterly sad old man. Edmund glances at his father and sees that he knows, but he still cannot help trying to warn his mother.

EDMUND

Mama! Stop talking. Why don't we go in to lunch.

MARY

Starts and at once the quality of unnatural detachment settles on her face again. She even smiles with an ironical amusement to herself.

Yes, it is inconsiderate of me to dig up the past, when I know your father and Jamie must be hungry.

Putting her arm around Edmund's shoulder—with a fond solicitude which is at the same time remote.

I do hope you have an appetite, dear. You really must eat more.

Her eyes become fixed on the whiskey glass on the table beside him—sharply.

Why is that glass there? Did you take a drink? Oh, how can you be such a fool? Don't you know it's the worst thing?

She turns on Tyrone.

You're to blame, James. How could you let him? Do you want to kill him? Don't you remember my father? He wouldn't stop after he was stricken. He said doctors were fools! He thought, like you, that whiskey is a good tonic!

A look of terror comes into her eyes and she stammers.

67

But, of course, there's no comparison at all. I don't know why I—
Forgive me for scolding you, James. One small drink won't hurt
Edmund. It might be good for him, if it gives him an appetite.

> *She pats Edmund's cheek playfully, the strange detachment
> again in her manner. He jerks his head away. She seems not
> to notice, but she moves instinctively away.*

JAMIE
> *Roughly, to hide his tense nerves.*

For God's sake, let's eat. I've been working in the damned dirt under
the hedge all morning. I've earned my grub.

> *He comes around in back of his father, not looking at his
> mother, and grabs Edmund's shoulder.*

Come on, Kid. Let's put on the feed bag.

> *Edmund gets up, keeping his eyes averted from his mother.
> They pass her, heading for the back parlor.*

TYRONE
> *Dully.*

Yes, you go in with your mother, lads. I'll join you in a second.

> *But they keep on without waiting for her. She looks at their
> backs with a helpless hurt and, as they enter the back parlor,
> starts to follow them. Tyrone's eyes are on her, sad and con-
> demning. She feels them and turns sharply without meeting
> his stare.*

MARY

Why do you look at me like that?

> *Her hands flutter up to pat her hair.*

Is it my hair coming down? I was so worn out from last night. I
thought I'd better lie down this morning. I drowsed off and had a
nice refreshing nap. But I'm sure I fixed my hair again when I woke
up.

> *Forcing a laugh.*

Although, as usual, I couldn't find my glasses.

> *Sharply.*

Please stop staring! One would think you were accusing me—

> *Then pleadingly.*

James! You don't understand!

TYRONE
With dull anger.
I understand that I've been a God-damned fool to believe in you!
He walks away from her to pour himself a big drink.

MARY
Her face again sets in stubborn defiance.
I don't know what you mean by "believing in me." All I've felt was
distrust and spying and suspicion.
Then accusingly.
Why are you having another drink? You never have more than one
before lunch.
Bitterly.
I know what to expect. You will be drunk tonight. Well, it won't
be the first time, will it—or the thousandth?
Again she bursts out pleadingly.
Oh, James, please! You don't understand! I'm so worried about Ed-
mund! I'm so afraid he—

TYRONE
I don't want to listen to your excuses, Mary.

MARY
Strickenly.
Excuses? You mean— ? Oh, you can't believe that of me! You
mustn't believe that, James!
*Then slipping away into her strange detachment—quite
casually.*
Shall we not go into lunch, dear? I don't want anything but I know
you're hungry.
*He walks slowly to where she stands in the doorway. He
walks like an old man. As he reaches her she bursts out
piteously.*
James! I tried so hard! I tried so hard! Please believe—!

TYRONE
Moved in spite of himself—helplessly.
I suppose you did, Mary.
Then grief-strickenly.
For the love of God, why couldn't you have the strength to keep on?

69

MARY
Her face setting into that stubborn denial again.
I don't know what you're talking about. Have the strength to keep
on what?

TYRONE
Hopelessly.
Never mind. It's no use now.
*He moves on and she keeps beside him as they disappear in
the back parlor.*

CURTAIN

Act Two, Scene Two

SCENE   *The same, about a half hour later. The tray with the bottle of whiskey has been removed from the table. The family are returning from lunch as the curtain rises. Mary is the first to enter from the back parlor. Her husband follows. He is not with her as he was in the similar entrance after breakfast at the opening of Act One. He avoids touching her or looking at her. There is condemnation in his face, mingled now with the beginning of an old weary, helpless resignation. Jamie and Edmund follow their father. Jamie's face is hard with defensive cynicism. Edmund tries to copy this defense but without success. He plainly shows he is heartsick as well as physically ill.*

Mary is terribly nervous again, as if the strain of sitting through lunch with them had been too much for her. Yet at the same time, in contrast to this, her expression shows more of that strange aloofness which seems to stand apart from her nerves and the anxieties which harry them.

She is talking as she enters—a stream of words that issues casually, in a routine of family conversation, from her mouth. She appears indifferent to the fact that their thoughts are not on what she is saying any more than her own are. As she talks, she comes to the left of the table and stands, facing front, one hand fumbling with the bosom of her dress, the other playing over the table top. Tyrone lights a cigar and goes to the screen door, staring out. Jamie fills a pipe from a jar on top of the bookcase at rear. He lights it as he goes to look out the window at right. Edmund sits in a chair by the table, turned half away from his mother so he does not have to watch her.

MARY

It's no use finding fault with Bridget. She doesn't listen. I can't threaten her, or she'd threaten she'd leave. And she does do her best

71

at times. It's too bad they seem to be just the times you're sure to be late, James. Well, there's this consolation: it's difficult to tell from her cooking whether she's doing her best or her worst.

She gives a little laugh of detached amusement—indifferently.
Never mind. The summer will soon be over, thank goodness. Your season will open again and we can go back to second-rate hotels and trains. I hate them, too, but at least I don't expect them to be like a home, and there's no housekeeping to worry about. It's unreasonable to expect Bridget or Cathleen to act as if this was a home. They know it isn't as well as we know it. It never has been and it never will be.

TYRONE
Bitterly without turning around.
No, it never can be now. But it was once, before you—

MARY
Her face instantly set in blank denial.
Before I what?
There is a dead silence. She goes on with a return of her detached air.
No, no. Whatever you mean, it isn't true, dear. It was never a home. You've always preferred the Club or a barroom. And for me it's always been as lonely as a dirty room in a one-night stand hotel. In a real home one is never lonely. You forget I know from experience what a home is like. I gave up one to marry you—my father's home.
At once, through an association of ideas she turns to Edmund. Her manner becomes tenderly solicitous, but there is the strange quality of detachment in it.
I'm worried about you, Edmund. You hardly touched a thing at lunch. That's no way to take care of yourself. It's all right for me not to have an appetite. I've been growing too fat. But you must eat.
Coaxingly maternal.
Promise me you will, dear, for my sake.

EDMUND
Dully.
Yes, Mama.

MARY

Pats his cheek as he tries not to shrink away.

That's a good boy.

There is another pause of dead silence. Then the telephone in the front hall rings and all of them stiffen startledly.

TYRONE

Hastily.

I'll answer. McGuire said he'd call me.

He goes out through the front parlor.

MARY

Indifferently.

McGuire. He must have another piece of property on his list that no one would think of buying except your father. It doesn't matter any more, but it's always seemed to me your father could afford to keep on buying property but never to give me a home.

She stops to listen as Tyrone's voice is heard from the hall.

TYRONE

Hello.

With forced heartiness.

Oh, how are you, Doctor?

Jamie turns from the window. Mary's fingers play more rapidly on the table top. Tyrone's voice, trying to conceal, reveals that he is hearing bad news.

I see—

Hurriedly.

Well, you'll explain all about it when you see him this afternoon. Yes, he'll be in without fail. Four o'clock. I'll drop in myself and have a talk with you before that. I have to go uptown on business, anyway. Goodbye, Doctor.

EDMUND

Dully.

That didn't sound like glad tidings.

Jamie gives him a pitying glance—then looks out the window again. Mary's face is terrified and her hands flutter distractedly. Tyrone comes in. The strain is obvious in his casualness as he addresses Edmund.

TYRONE

It was Doctor Hardy. He wants you to be sure and see him at four.

EDMUND

Dully.

What did he say? Not that I give a damn now.

MARY

Bursts out excitedly.

I wouldn't believe him if he swore on a stack of Bibles. You mustn't pay attention to a word he says, Edmund.

TYRONE

Sharply.

Mary!

MARY

More excitedly.

Oh, we all realize why you like him, James! Because he's cheap! But please don't try to tell me! I know all about Doctor Hardy. Heaven knows I ought to after all these years. He's an ignorant fool! There should be a law to keep men like him from practicing. He hasn't the slightest idea— When you're in agony and half insane, he sits and holds your hand and delivers sermons on will power!

> *Her face is drawn in an expression of intense suffering by the memory. For the moment, she loses all caution. With bitter hatred.*

He deliberately humiliates you! He makes you beg and plead! He treats you like a criminal! He understands nothing! And yet it was exactly the same type of cheap quack who first gave you the medicine—and you never knew what it was until too late!

> *Passionately.*

I hate doctors! They'll do anything—anything to keep you coming to them. They'll sell their souls! What's worse, they'll sell yours, and you never know it till one day you find yourself in hell!

EDMUND

Mama! For God's sake, stop talking.

TYRONE

Shakenly.

Yes, Mary, it's no time—

MARY

Suddenly is overcome by guilty confusion—stammers.

I— Forgive me, dear. You're right. It's useless to be angry now.

*There is again a pause of dead silence. When she speaks
again, her face has cleared and is calm, and the quality of
uncanny detachment is in her voice and manner.*

I'm going upstairs for a moment, if you'll excuse me. I have to fix
my hair.

She adds smilingly.

That is if I can find my glasses. I'll be right down.

TYRONE

As she starts through the doorway—pleading and rebuking.

Mary!

MARY

Turns to stare at him calmly.

Yes, dear? What is it?

TYRONE

Helplessly.

Nothing.

MARY

With a strange derisive smile.

You're welcome to come up and watch me if you're so suspicious.

TYRONE

As if that could do any good! You'd only postpone it. And I'm not
your jailor. This isn't a prison.

MARY

No. I know you can't help thinking it's a home.

She adds quickly with a detached contrition.

I'm sorry, dear. I don't mean to be bitter. It's not your fault.

*She turns and disappears through the back parlor. The three
in the room remain silent. It is as if they were waiting until
she got upstairs before speaking.*

JAMIE

Cynically brutal.

Another shot in the arm!

EDMUND
Angrily.
Cut out that kind of talk!

TYRONE
Yes! Hold your foul tongue and your rotten Broadway loafer's lingo! Have you no pity or decency?
Losing his temper.
You ought to be kicked out in the gutter! But if I did it, you know damned well who'd weep and plead for you, and excuse you and complain till I let you come back.

JAMIE
A spasm of pain crosses his face.
Christ, don't I know that? No pity? I have all the pity in the world for her. I understand what a hard game to beat she's up against—which is more than you ever have! My lingo didn't mean I had no feeling. I was merely putting bluntly what we all know, and have to live with now, again.
Bitterly.
The cures are no damned good except for a while. The truth is there is no cure and we've been saps to hope—
Cynically.
They never come back!

EDMUND
Scornfully parodying his brother's cynicism.
They never come back! Everything is in the bag! It's all a frame-up! We're all fall guys and suckers and we can't beat the game!
Disdainfully.
Christ, if I felt the way you do—!

JAMIE
Stung for a moment—then shrugging his shoulders, dryly.
I thought you did. Your poetry isn't very cheery. Nor the stuff you read and claim you admire.
He indicates the small bookcase at rear.
Your pet with the unpronounceable name, for example.

EDMUND

Nietzsche. You don't know what you're talking about. You haven't read him.

JAMIE

Enough to know it's a lot of bunk!

TYRONE

Shut up, both of you! There's little choice between the philosophy you learned from Broadway loafers, and the one Edmund got from his books. They're both rotten to the core. You've both flouted the faith you were born and brought up in—the one true faith of the Catholic Church—and your denial has brought nothing but self-destruction!

His two sons stare at him contemptuously. They forget their quarrel and are as one against him on this issue.

EDMUND

That's the bunk, Papa!

JAMIE

We don't pretend, at any rate.
Caustically.
I don't notice you've worn any holes in the knees of your pants going to Mass.

TYRONE

It's true I'm a bad Catholic in the observance, God forgive me. But I believe!
Angrily.
And you're a liar! I may not go to church but every night and morning of my life I get on my knees and pray!

EDMUND

Bitingly.
Did you pray for Mama?

TYRONE

I did. I've prayed to God these many years for her.

EDMUND

Then Nietzsche must be right.

77

He quotes from Thus Spake Zarathustra.
"God is dead: of His pity for man hath God died."

TYRONE
Ignores this.
If your mother had prayed, too— She hasn't denied her faith, but she's forgotten it, until now there's no strength of the spirit left in her to fight against her curse.
Then dully resigned.
But what's the good of talk? We've lived with this before and now we must again. There's no help for it.
Bitterly.
Only I wish she hadn't led me to hope this time. By God, I never will again!

EDMUND
That's a rotten thing to say, Papa!
Defiantly.
Well, I'll hope! She's just started. It can't have got a hold on her yet. She can still stop. I'm going to talk to her.

JAMIE
Shrugs his shoulders.
You can't talk to her now. She'll listen but she won't listen. She'll be here but she won't be here. You know the way she gets.

TYRONE
Yes, that's the way the poison acts on her always. Every day from now on, there'll be the same drifting away from us until by the end of each night—

EDMUND
Miserably.
Cut it out, Papa!
He jumps up from his chair.
I'm going to get dressed.
Bitterly, as he goes.
I'll make so much noise she can't suspect I've come to spy on her.
He disappears through the front parlor and can be heard stamping noisily upstairs.

JAMIE
After a pause.
What did Doc Hardy say about the Kid?

TYRONE
Dully.
It's what you thought. He's got consumption.

JAMIE
God damn it!

TYRONE
There is no possible doubt, he said.

JAMIE
He'll have to go to a sanatorium.

TYRONE
Yes, and the sooner the better, Hardy said, for him and everyone
around him. He claims that in six months to a year Edmund will be
cured, if he obeys orders.
He sighs—gloomily and resentfully.
I never thought a child of mine— It doesn't come from my side of
the family. There wasn't one of us that didn't have lungs as strong
as an ox.

JAMIE
Who gives a damn about that part of it! Where does Hardy want to
send him?

TYRONE
That's what I'm to see him about.

JAMIE
Well, for God's sake, pick out a good place and not some cheap
dump!

TYRONE
Stung.
I'll send him wherever Hardy thinks best!

JAMIE
Well, don't give Hardy your old over-the-hills-to-the-poorhouse
song about taxes and mortgages.

TYRONE

I'm no millionaire who can throw money away! Why shouldn't I tell Hardy the truth?

JAMIE

Because he'll think you want him to pick a cheap dump, and because he'll know it isn't the truth—especially if he hears afterwards you've seen McGuire and let that flannel-mouth, gold-brick merchant sting you with another piece of bum property!

TYRONE
Furiously.

Keep your nose out of my business!

JAMIE

This is Edmund's business. What I'm afraid of is, with your Irish bog-trotter idea that consumption is fatal, you'll figure it would be a waste of money to spend any more than you can help.

TYRONE

You liar!

JAMIE

All right. Prove I'm a liar. That's what I want. That's why I brought it up.

TYRONE
His rage still smouldering.

I have every hope Edmund will be cured. And keep your dirty tongue off Ireland! You're a fine one to sneer, with the map of it on your face!

JAMIE

Not after I wash my face.
Then before his father can react to this insult to the Old Sod, he adds dryly, shrugging his shoulders.
Well, I've said all I have to say. It's up to you.
Abruptly.
What do you want me to do this afternoon, now you're going up-town? I've done all I can do on the hedge until you cut more of it. You don't want me to go ahead with your clipping, I know that.

TYRONE

No. You'd get it crooked, as you get everything else.

JAMIE

Then I'd better go uptown with Edmund. The bad news coming on top of what's happened to Mama may hit him hard.

TYRONE

Forgetting his quarrel.

Yes, go with him, Jamie. Keep up his spirits, if you can.

He adds caustically.

If you can without making it an excuse to get drunk!

JAMIE

What would I use for money? The last I heard they were still selling booze, not giving it away.

He starts for the front-parlor doorway.

I'll get dressed.

He stops in the doorway as he sees his mother approaching from the hall, and moves aside to let her come in. Her eyes look brighter, and her manner is more detached. This change becomes more marked as the scene goes on.

MARY

Vaguely.

You haven't seen my glasses anywhere, have you, Jamie?

She doesn't look at him. He glances away, ignoring her question but she doesn't seem to expect an answer. She comes forward, addressing her husband without looking at him.

You haven't seen them, have you, James?

Behind her Jamie disappears through the front parlor.

TYRONE

Turns to look out the screen door.

No, Mary.

MARY

What's the matter with Jamie? Have you been nagging at him again? You shouldn't treat him with such contempt all the time. He's not to blame. If he'd been brought up in a real home, I'm sure he would have been different.

She comes to the windows at right—lightly.

You're not much of a weather prophet, dear. See how hazy it's getting. I can hardly see the other shore.

TYRONE
Trying to speak naturally.

Yes, I spoke too soon. We're in for another night of fog, I'm afraid.

MARY

Oh, well, I won't mind it tonight.

TYRONE

No, I don't imagine you will, Mary.

MARY
Flashes a glance at him—after a pause.

I don't see Jamie going down to the hedge. Where did he go?

TYRONE

He's going with Edmund to the Doctor's. He went up to change his clothes.
Then, glad of an excuse to leave her.

I'd better do the same or I'll be late for my appointment at the Club.
He makes a move toward the front-parlor doorway, but with a swift impulsive movement she reaches out and clasps his arm.

MARY
A note of pleading in her voice.

Don't go yet, dear. I don't want to be alone.
Hastily.

I mean, you have plenty of time. You know you boast you can dress in one-tenth the time it takes the boys.
Vaguely.

There is something I wanted to say. What is it? I've forgotten. I'm glad Jamie is going uptown. You didn't give him any money, I hope.

TYRONE

I did not.

MARY

He'd only spend it on drink and you know what a vile, poisonous tongue he has when he's drunk. Not that I would mind anything he said tonight, but he always manages to drive you into a rage, especially if you're drunk, too, as you will be.

TYRONE
Resentfully.
I won't. I never get drunk.

MARY
Teasing indifferently.
Oh, I'm sure you'll hold it well. You always have. It's hard for a stranger to tell, but after thirty-five years of marriage—

TYRONE
I've never missed a performance in my life. That's the proof!
Then bitterly.
If I did get drunk it is not you who should blame me. No man has ever had a better reason.

MARY
Reason? What reason? You always drink too much when you go to the Club, don't you? Particularly when you meet McGuire. He sees to that. Don't think I'm finding fault, dear. You must do as you please. I won't mind.

TYRONE
I know you won't.
He turns toward the front parlor, anxious to escape.
I've got to get dressed.

MARY
Again she reaches out and grasps his arm—pleadingly.
No, please wait a little while, dear. At least, until one of the boys comes down. You will all be leaving me so soon.

TYRONE
With bitter sadness.
It's you who are leaving us, Mary.

MARY
I? That's a silly thing to say, James. How could I leave? There is nowhere I could go. Who would I go to see? I have no friends.

TYRONE

It's your own fault—

He stops and sighs helplessly—persuasively.

There's surely one thing you can do this afternoon that will be good for you, Mary. Take a drive in the automobile. Get away from the house. Get a little sun and fresh air.

Injuredly.

I bought the automobile for you. You know I don't like the damned things. I'd rather walk any day, or take a trolley.

With growing resentment.

I had it here waiting for you when you came back from the sanatorium. I hoped it would give you pleasure and distract your mind. You used to ride in it every day, but you've hardly used it at all lately. I paid a lot of money I couldn't afford, and there's the chauffeur I have to board and lodge and pay high wages whether he drives you or not.

Bitterly.

Waste! The same old waste that will land me in the poorhouse in my old age! What good did it do you? I might as well have thrown the money out the window.

MARY

With detached calm.

Yes, it was a waste of money, James. You shouldn't have bought a secondhand automobile. You were swindled again as you always are, because you insist on secondhand bargains in everything.

TYRONE

It's one of the best makes! Everyone says it's better than any of the new ones!

MARY

Ignoring this.

It was another waste to hire Smythe, who was only a helper in a garage and had never been a chauffeur. Oh, I realize his wages are less than a real chauffeur's, but he more than makes up for that, I'm sure, by the graft he gets from the garage on repair bills. Something is always wrong. Smythe sees to that, I'm afraid.

TYRONE

I don't believe it! He may not be a fancy millionaire's flunky but he's honest! You're as bad as Jamie, suspecting everyone!

MARY

You mustn't be offended, dear. I wasn't offended when you gave me the automobile. I knew you didn't mean to humiliate me. I knew that was the way you had to do everything. I was grateful and touched. I knew buying the car was a hard thing for you to do, and it proved how much you loved me, in your way, especially when you couldn't really believe it would do me any good.

TYRONE

Mary!
> *He suddenly hugs her to him—brokenly.*

Dear Mary! For the love of God, for my sake and the boys' sake and your own, won't you stop now?

MARY
> *Stammers in guilty confusion for a second.*

I— James! Please!
> *Her strange, stubborn defense comes back instantly.*

Stop what? What are you talking about?
> *He lets his arm fall to his side brokenly. She impulsively puts her arm around him.*

James! We've loved each other! We always will! Let's remember only that, and not try to understand what we cannot understand, or help things that cannot be helped—the things life has done to us we cannot excuse or explain.

TYRONE
> *As if he hadn't heard—bitterly.*

You won't even try?

MARY
> *Her arms drop hopelessly and she turns away—with detachment.*

Try to go for a drive this afternoon, you mean? Why, yes, if you wish me to, although it makes me feel lonelier than if I stayed here. There is no one I can invite to drive with me, and I never know where to tell Smythe to go. If there was a friend's house where I could drop in and laugh and gossip awhile. But, of course, there isn't. There never has been.

> *Her manner becoming more and more remote.*

At the Convent I had so many friends. Girls whose families lived in lovely homes. I used to visit them and they'd visit me in my father's home. But, naturally, after I married an actor—you know how actors were considered in those days—a lot of them gave me the cold shoulder. And then, right after we were married, there was the scandal of that woman who had been your mistress, suing you. From then on, all my old friends either pitied me or cut me dead. I hated the ones who cut me much less than the pitiers.

TYRONE
> *With guilty resentment.*

For God's sake, don't dig up what's long forgotten. If you're that far gone in the past already, when it's only the beginning of the afternoon, what will you be tonight?

MARY
> *Stares at him defiantly now.*

Come to think of it, I do have to drive uptown. There's something I must get at the drugstore.

TYRONE
> *Bitterly scornful.*

Leave it to you to have some of the stuff hidden, and prescriptions for more! I hope you'll lay in a good stock ahead so we'll never have another night like the one when you screamed for it, and ran out of the house in your nightdress half crazy, to try and throw yourself off the dock!

MARY
> *Tries to ignore this.*

I have to get tooth powder and toilet soap and cold cream—
> *She breaks down pitiably.*

James! You mustn't remember! You mustn't humiliate me so!

TYRONE
> *Ashamed.*

I'm sorry. Forgive me, Mary!

MARY

Defensively detached again.

It doesn't matter. Nothing like that ever happened. You must have dreamed it.

He stares at her hopelessly. Her voice seems to drift farther and farther away.

I was so healthy before Edmund was born. You remember, James. There wasn't a nerve in my body. Even traveling with you season after season, with week after week of one-night stands, in trains without Pullmans, in dirty rooms of filthy hotels, eating bad food, bearing children in hotel rooms, I still kept healthy. But bearing Edmund was the last straw. I was so sick afterwards, and that ignorant quack of a cheap hotel doctor— All he knew was I was in pain. It was easy for him to stop the pain.

TYRONE

Mary! For God's sake, forget the past!

MARY

With strange objective calm.

Why? How can I? The past is the present, isn't it? It's the future, too. We all try to lie out of that but life won't let us.

Going on.

I blame only myself. I swore after Eugene died I would never have another baby. I was to blame for his death. If I hadn't left him with my mother to join you on the road, because you wrote telling me you missed me and were so lonely, Jamie would never have been allowed, when he still had measles, to go in the baby's room.

Her face hardening.

I've always believed Jamie did it on purpose. He was jealous of the baby. He hated him.

As Tyrone starts to protest.

Oh, I know Jamie was only seven, but he was never stupid. He'd been warned it might kill the baby. He knew. I've never been able to forgive him for that.

TYRONE

With bitter sadness.

Are you back with Eugene now? Can't you let our dead baby rest in peace?

MARY

As if she hadn't heard him.

It was my fault. I should have insisted on staying with Eugene and not have let you persuade me to join you, just because I loved you. Above all, I shouldn't have let you insist I have another baby to take Eugene's place, because you thought that would make me forget his death. I knew from experience by then that children should have homes to be born in, if they are to be good children, and women need homes, if they are to be good mothers. I was afraid all the time I carried Edmund. I knew something terrible would happen. I knew I'd proved by the way I'd left Eugene that I wasn't worthy to have another baby, and that God would punish me if I did. I never should have borne Edmund.

TYRONE

With an uneasy glance through the front parlor.

Mary! Be careful with your talk. If he heard you he might think you never wanted him. He's feeling bad enough already without—

MARY

Violently.

It's a lie! I did want him! More than anything in the world! You don't understand! I meant, for his sake. He has never been happy. He never will be. Nor healthy. He was born nervous and too sensitive, and that's my fault. And now, ever since he's been so sick I've kept remembering Eugene and my father and I've been so frightened and guilty—

Then, catching herself, with an instant change to stubborn denial.

Oh, I know it's foolish to imagine dreadful things when there's no reason for it. After all, everyone has colds and gets over them.

Tyrone stares at her and sighs helplessly. He turns away toward the front parlor and sees Edmund coming down the stairs in the hall.

TYRONE

Sharply, in a low voice.

Here's Edmund. For God's sake try and be yourself—at least until he goes! You can do that much for him!

He waits, forcing his face into a pleasantly paternal expression. She waits frightenedly, seized again by a nervous panic, her hands fluttering over the bosom of her dress, up to her throat and hair, with a distracted aimlessness. Then, as Edmund approaches the doorway, she cannot face him. She goes swiftly away to the windows at left and stares out with her back to the front parlor. Edmund enters. He has changed to a ready-made blue serge suit, high stiff collar and tie, black shoes.

With an actor's heartiness.

Well! You look spic and span. I'm on my way up to change, too.

He starts to pass him.

EDMUND

Dryly.

Wait a minute, Papa. I hate to bring up disagreeable topics, but there's the matter of carfare. I'm broke.

TYRONE

Starts automatically on a customary lecture.

You'll always be broke until you learn the value—

Checks himself guiltily, looking at his son's sick face with worried pity.

But you've been learning, lad. You worked hard before you took ill. You've done splendidly. I'm proud of you.

He pulls out a small roll of bills from his pants pocket and carefully selects one. Edmund takes it. He glances at it and his face expresses astonishment. His father again reacts customarily—sarcastically.

Thank you.

He quotes.

"How sharper than a serpent's tooth it is—"

EDMUND

"To have a thankless child." I know. Give me a chance, Papa. I'm knocked speechless. This isn't a dollar. It's a ten spot.

TYRONE

Embarrassed by his generosity.

Put it in your pocket. You'll probably meet some of your friends uptown and you can't hold your end up and be sociable with nothing in your jeans.

EDMUND

You meant it? Gosh, thank you, Papa.

He is genuinely pleased and grateful for a moment—then he stares at his father's face with uneasy suspicion.

But why all of a sudden—?

Cynically.

Did Doc Hardy tell you I was going to die?

Then he sees his father is bitterly hurt.

No! That's a rotten crack. I was only kidding, Papa.

He puts an arm around his father impulsively and gives him an affectionate hug.

I'm very grateful. Honest, Papa.

TYRONE

Touched, returns his hug.

You're welcome, lad.

MARY

Suddenly turns to them in a confused panic of frightened anger.

I won't have it!

She stamps her foot.

Do you hear, Edmund! Such morbid nonsense! Saying you're going to die! It's the books you read! Nothing but sadness and death! Your father shouldn't allow you to have them. And some of the poems you've written yourself are even worse! You'd think you didn't want to live! A boy of your age with everything before him! It's just a pose you get out of books! You're not really sick at all!

TYRONE

Mary! Hold your tongue!

MARY

Instantly changing to a detached tone.

But, James, it's absurd of Edmund to be so gloomy and make such a great to-do about nothing.

Turning to Edmund but avoiding his eyes—teasingly af-
fectionate.

Never mind, dear. I'm on to you.

She comes to him.

You want to be petted and spoiled and made a fuss over, isn't that
it? You're still such a baby.

She puts her arm around him and hugs him. He remains
rigid and unyielding. Her voice begins to tremble.

But please don't carry it too far, dear. Don't say horrible things. I
know it's foolish to take them seriously but I can't help it. You've
got me—so frightened.

She breaks and hides her face on his shoulder, sobbing. Ed-
mund is moved in spite of himself. He pats her shoulder with
an awkward tenderness.

EDMUND

Don't, mother.

His eyes meet his father's.

TYRONE

Huskily—clutching at hopeless hope.

Maybe if you asked your mother now what you said you were going
to—

He fumbles with his watch.

By God, look at the time! I'll have to shake a leg.

He hurries away through the front parlor. Mary lifts her
head. Her manner is again one of detached motherly solici-
tude. She seems to have forgotten the tears which are still in
her eyes.

MARY

How do you feel, dear?

She feels his forehead.

Your head is a little hot, but that's just from going out in the sun.
You look ever so much better than you did this morning.

Taking his hand.

Come and sit down. You mustn't stand on your feet so much. You
must learn to husband your strength.

She gets him to sit and she sits sideways on the arm of his chair, an arm around his shoulder, so he cannot meet her eyes.

EDMUND

Starts to blurt out the appeal he now feels is quite hopeless.

Listen, Mama—

MARY

Interrupting quickly.

Now, now! Don't talk. Lean back and rest.

Persuasively.

You know, I think it would be much better for you if you stayed home this afternoon and let me take care of you. It's such a tiring trip uptown in the dirty old trolley on a hot day like this. I'm sure you'd be much better off here with me.

EDMUND

Dully.

You forget I have an appointment with Hardy.

Trying again to get his appeal started.

Listen, Mama—

MARY

Quickly.

You can telephone and say you don't feel well enough.

Excitedly.

It's simply a waste of time and money seeing him. He'll only tell you some lie. He'll pretend he's found something serious the matter because that's his bread and butter.

She gives a hard sneering little laugh.

The old idiot! All he knows about medicine is to look solemn and preach will power!

EDMUND

Trying to catch her eyes.

Mama! Please listen! I want to ask you something! You— You're only just started. You can still stop. You've got the will power! We'll all help you. I'll do anything! Won't you, Mama?

MARY

Stammers pleadingly.

Please don't—talk about things you don't understand!

EDMUND

Dully.

All right, I give up. I knew it was no use.

MARY

In blank denial now.

Anyway, I don't know what you're referring to. But I do know you should be the last one— Right after I returned from the sanatorium, you began to be ill. The doctor there had warned me I must have peace at home with nothing to upset me, and all I've done is worry about you.

Then distractedly.

But that's no excuse! I'm only trying to explain. It's not an excuse!

She hugs him to her—pleadingly.

Promise me, dear, you won't believe I made you an excuse.

EDMUND

Bitterly.

What else can I believe?

MARY

Slowly takes her arm away—her manner remote and objective again.

Yes, I suppose you can't help suspecting that.

EDMUND

Ashamed but still bitter.

What do you expect?

MARY

Nothing, I don't blame you. How could you believe me—when I can't believe myself? I've become such a liar. I never lied about anything once upon a time. Now I have to lie, especially to myself. But how can you understand, when I don't myself. I've never understood anything about it, except that one day long ago I found I could no longer call my soul my own.

She pauses—then lowering her voice to a strange tone of whispered confidence.

But some day, dear, I will find it again—some day when you're all well, and I see you healthy and happy and successful, and I don't have to feel guilty any more—some day when the Blessed Virgin Mary forgives me and gives me back the faith in Her love and pity I used to have in my convent days, and I can pray to Her again—when She sees no one in the world can believe in me even for a moment any more, then She will believe in me, and with Her help it will be so easy. I will hear myself scream with agony, and at the same time I will laugh because I will be so sure of myself.

> *Then as Edmund remains hopelessly silent, she adds sadly.*

Of course, you can't believe that, either.

> *She rises from the arm of his chair and goes to stare out the windows at right with her back to him—casually.*

Now I think of it, you might as well go uptown. I forgot I'm taking a drive. I have to go to the drugstore. You would hardly want to go there with me. You'd be so ashamed.

EDMUND
Brokenly.

Mama! Don't!

MARY

I suppose you'll divide that ten dollars your father gave you with Jamie. You always divide with each other, don't you? Like good sports. Well, I know what he'll do with his share. Get drunk someplace where he can be with the only kind of woman he understands or likes.

> *She turns to him, pleading frightenedly.*

Edmund! Promise me you won't drink! It's so dangerous! You know Doctor Hardy told you—

EDMUND
Bitterly.

I thought he was an old idiot.

MARY
Pitifully.

Edmund!

> *Jamie's voice is heard from the front hall,*
> "Come on, Kid, let's beat it."
> *Mary's manner at once becomes detached again.*

Go on, Edmund. Jamie's waiting.

She goes to the front-parlor doorway.
There comes your father downstairs, too.
Tyrone's voice calls,
"Come on, Edmund."

MARY
Kisses him with detached affection.
Goodbye, dear. If you're coming home for dinner, try not to be late.
And tell your father. You know what Bridget is.
He turns and hurries away. Tyrone calls from the hall,
"Goodbye, Mary," and then Jamie, "Goodbye, Mama."
She calls back.
Goodbye.
The front screen door is heard closing after them. She comes
and stands by the table, one hand drumming on it, the other
fluttering up to pat her hair. She stares about the room with
frightened, forsaken eyes and whispers to herself.
It's so lonely here.
Then her face hardens into bitter self-contempt.
You're lying to yourself again. You wanted to get rid of them. Their
contempt and disgust aren't pleasant company. You're glad they're
gone.
She gives a little despairing laugh.
Then Mother of God, why do I feel so lonely?

CURTAIN

Act Three

The same. It is around half past six in the evening. Dusk is gathering in the living room, an early dusk due to the fog which has rolled in from the Sound and is like a white curtain drawn down outside the windows. From a lighthouse beyond the harbor's mouth, a foghorn is heard at regular intervals, moaning like a mournful whale in labor, and from the harbor itself, intermittently, comes the warning ringing of bells on yachts at anchor.

The tray with the bottle of whiskey, glasses, and pitcher of ice water is on the table, as it was in the pre-luncheon scene of the previous act.

Mary and the second girl, Cathleen, are discovered. The latter is standing at left of table. She holds an empty whiskey glass in her hand as if she'd forgotten she had it. She shows the effects of drink. Her stupid, good-humored face wears a pleased and flattered simper.

Mary is paler than before and her eyes shine with unnatural brilliance. The strange detachment in her manner has intensified. She has hidden deeper within herself and found refuge and release in a dream where present reality is but an appearance to be accepted and dismissed unfeelingly—even with a hard cynicism—or entirely ignored. There is at times an uncanny gay, free youthfulness in her manner, as if in spirit she were released to become again, simply and without self-consciousness, the naive, happy, chattering schoolgirl of her convent days. She wears the dress into which she had changed for her drive to town, a simple, fairly expensive affair, which would be extremely becoming if it were not for the careless, almost slovenly way she wears it. Her hair is no longer fastidiously in place. It has a slightly disheveled, lopsided look. She talks to Cathleen with a confiding fa-

miliarity, as if the second girl were an old, intimate friend. As the curtain rises, she is standing by the screen door looking out. A moan of the foghorn is heard.

MARY
Amused—girlishly.
That foghorn! Isn't it awful, Cathleen?

CATHLEEN
Talks more familiarly than usual but never with intentional impertinence because she sincerely likes her mistress.
It is indeed, Ma'am. It's like a banshee.

MARY
Goes on as if she hadn't heard. In nearly all the following dialogue there is the feeling that she has Cathleen with her merely as an excuse to keep talking.
I don't mind it tonight. Last night it drove me crazy. I lay awake worrying until I couldn't stand it any more.

CATHLEEN
Bad cess to it. I was scared out of my wits riding back from town. I thought that ugly monkey, Smythe, would drive us in a ditch or against a tree. You couldn't see your hand in front of you. I'm glad you had me sit in back with you, Ma'am. If I'd been in front with that monkey— He can't keep his dirty hands to himself. Give him half a chance and he's pinching me on the leg or you-know-where— asking your pardon, Ma'am, but it's true.

MARY
Dreamily.
It wasn't the fog I minded, Cathleen. I really love fog.

CATHLEEN
They say it's good for the complexion.

MARY
It hides you from the world and the world from you. You feel that everything has changed, and nothing is what it seemed to be. No one can find or touch you any more.

98

CATHLEEN

I wouldn't care so much if Smythe was a fine, handsome man like some chauffeurs I've seen—I mean, if it was all in fun, for I'm a decent girl. But for a shriveled runt like Smythe—! I've told him, you must think I'm hard up that I'd notice a monkey like you. I've warned him, one day I'll give a clout that'll knock him into next week. And so I will!

MARY

It's the foghorn I hate. It won't let you alone. It keeps reminding you, and warning you, and calling you back.

She smiles strangely.

But it can't tonight. It's just an ugly sound. It doesn't remind me of anything.

She gives a teasing, girlish laugh.

Except, perhaps, Mr. Tyrone's snores. I've always had such fun teasing him about it. He has snored ever since I can remember, especially when he's had too much to drink, and yet he's like a child, he hates to admit it.

She laughs, coming to the table.

Well, I suppose I snore at times, too, and I don't like to admit it. So I have no right to make fun of him, have I?

She sits in the rocker at right of table.

CATHLEEN

Ah, sure, everybody healthy snores. It's a sign of sanity, they say.

Then, worriedly.

What time is it, Ma'am? I ought to go back in the kitchen. The damp is in Bridget's rheumatism and she's like a raging divil. She'll bite my head off.

She puts her glass on the table and makes a movement toward the back parlor.

MARY

With a flash of apprehension.

No, don't go, Cathleen. I don't want to be alone, yet.

CATHLEEN

You won't be for long. The Master and the boys will be home soon.

MARY

I doubt if they'll come back for dinner. They have too good an excuse to remain in the barrooms where they feel at home.

> *Cathleen stares at her, stupidly puzzled. Mary goes on
> smilingly.*

Don't worry about Bridget. I'll tell her I kept you with me, and you
can take a big drink of whiskey to her when you go. She won't
mind then.

CATHLEEN

> *Grins—at her ease again.*

No, Ma'am. That's the one thing can make her cheerful. She loves
her drop.

MARY

Have another drink yourself, if you wish, Cathleen.

CATHLEEN

I don't know if I'd better, Ma'am. I can feel what I've had already.

> *Reaching for the bottle.*

Well, maybe one more won't harm.

> *She pours a drink.*

Here's your good health, Ma'am.

> *She drinks without bothering about a chaser.*

MARY

> *Dreamily.*

I really did have good health once, Cathleen. But that was long ago.

CATHLEEN

> *Worried again.*

The Master's sure to notice what's gone from the bottle. He has the
eye of a hawk for that.

MARY

> *Amusedly.*

Oh, we'll play Jamie's trick on him. Just measure a few drinks of
water and pour them in.

CATHLEEN

> *Does this—with a silly giggle.*

God save me, it'll be half water. He'll know by the taste.

MARY

Indifferently.

No, by the time he comes home he'll be too drunk to tell the difference. He has such a good excuse, he believes, to drown his sorrows.

CATHLEEN

Philosophically.

Well, it's a good man's failing. I wouldn't give a trauneen for a teetotaler. They've no high spirits.

Then, stupidly puzzled.

Good excuse? You mean Master Edmund, Ma'am? I can tell the Master is worried about him.

MARY

Stiffens defensively—but in a strange way the reaction has a mechanical quality, as if it did not penetrate to real emotion.

Don't be silly, Cathleen. Why should he be? A touch of grippe is nothing. And Mr. Tyrone never is worried about anything, except money and property and the fear he'll end his days in poverty. I mean, deeply worried. Because he cannot really understand anything else.

She gives a little laugh of detached, affectionate amusement.

My husband is a very peculiar man, Cathleen.

CATHLEEN

Vaguely resentful.

Well, he's a fine, handsome, kind gentleman just the same, Ma'am. Never mind his weakness.

MARY

Oh, I don't mind. I've loved him dearly for thirty-six years. That proves I know he's lovable at heart and can't help being what he is, doesn't it?

CATHLEEN

Hazily reassured.

That's right, Ma'am. Love him dearly, for any fool can see he worships the ground you walk on.

Fighting the effect of her last drink and trying to be soberly conversational.

Speaking of acting, Ma'am, how is it you never went on the stage?

MARY

Resentfully.

I? What put that absurd notion in your head? I was brought up in a respectable home and educated in the best convent in the Middle West. Before I met Mr. Tyrone I hardly knew there was such a thing as a theater. I was a very pious girl. I even dreamed of becoming a nun. I've never had the slightest desire to be an actress.

CATHLEEN

Bluntly.

Well, I can't imagine you a holy nun, Ma'am. Sure, you never darken the door of a church, God forgive you.

MARY

Ignores this.

I've never felt at home in the theater. Even though Mr. Tyrone has made me go with him on all his tours, I've had little to do with the people in his company, or with anyone on the stage. Not that I have anything against them. They have always been kind to me, and I to them. But I've never felt at home with them. Their life is not my life. It has always stood between me and—

She gets up—abruptly.

But let's not talk of old things that couldn't be helped.

She goes to the porch door and stares out.

How thick the fog is. I can't see the road. All the people in the world could pass by and I would never know. I wish it was always that way. It's getting dark already. It will soon be night, thank goodness.

She turns back—vaguely.

It was kind of you to keep me company this afternoon, Cathleen. I would have been lonely driving uptown alone.

CATHLEEN

Sure, wouldn't I rather ride in a fine automobile than stay here and listen to Bridget's lies about her relations? It was like a vacation, Ma'am.

She pauses—then stupidly.

There was only one thing I didn't like.

MARY

Vaguely.

What was that, Cathleen?

The way the man in the drugstore acted when I took in the prescription for you.

Indignantly.

The impidence of him!

MARY

With stubborn blankness.

What are you talking about? What drugstore? What prescription?

Then hastily, as Cathleen stares in stupid amazement.

Oh, of course, I'd forgotten. The medicine for the rheumatism in my hands. What did the man say?

Then with indifference.

Not that it matters, as long as he filled the prescription.

CATHLEEN

It mattered to me, then! I'm not used to being treated like a thief. He gave me a long look and says insultingly, "Where did you get hold of this?" and I says, "It's none of your damned business, but if you must know, it's for the lady I work for, Mrs. Tyrone, who's sitting out in the automobile." That shut him up quick. He gave a look out at you and said, "Oh," and went to get the medicine.

MARY

Vaguely.

Yes, he knows me.

She sits in the armchair at right rear of table. She adds in a calm, detached voice.

I have to take it because there is no other that can stop the pain— all the pain—I mean, in my hands.

She raises her hands and regards them with melancholy sympathy. There is no tremor in them now.

Poor hands! You'd never believe it, but they were once one of my good points, along with my hair and eyes, and I had a fine figure, too.

Her tone has become more and more far-off and dreamy.

They were a musician's hands. I used to love the piano. I worked so hard at my music in the Convent—if you can call it work when you do something you love. Mother Elizabeth and my music teacher both said I had more talent than any student they remembered. My father paid for special lessons. He spoiled me. He would do anything I asked. He would have sent me to Europe to study after I graduated from the Convent. I might have gone—if I hadn't fallen in love with Mr. Tyrone. Or I might have become a nun. I had two dreams. To be a nun, that was the more beautiful one. To become a concert pianist, that was the other.

> *She pauses, regarding her hands fixedly. Cathleen blinks her eyes to fight off drowsiness and a tipsy feeling.*

I haven't touched a piano in so many years. I couldn't play with such crippled fingers, even if I wanted to. For a time after my marriage I tried to keep up my music. But it was hopeless. One-night stands, cheap hotels, dirty trains, leaving children, never having a home—

> *She stares at her hands with fascinated disgust.*

See, Cathleen, how ugly they are! So maimed and crippled! You would think they'd been through some horrible accident!

> *She gives a strange little laugh.*

So they have, come to think of it.

> *She suddenly thrusts her hands behind her back.*

I won't look at them. They're worse than the foghorn for reminding me—

> *Then with defiant self-assurance.*

But even they can't touch me now.

> *She brings her hands from behind her back and deliberately stares at them—calmly.*

They're far away. I see them, but the pain has gone.

CATHLEEN
> *Stupidly puzzled.*

You've taken some of the medicine? It made you act funny, Ma'am. If I didn't know better, I'd think you'd a drop taken.

MARY
> *Dreamily.*

It kills the pain. You go back until at last you are beyond its reach. Only the past when you were happy is real.

> *She pauses—then as if her words had been an evocation which called back happiness she changes in her whole manner*

and facial expression. She looks younger. There is a quality
of an innocent convent girl about her, and she smiles shyly.
If you think Mr. Tyrone is handsome now, Cathleen, you should
have seen him when I first met him. He had the reputation of being
one of the best looking men in the country. The girls in the Convent
who had seen him act, or seen his photographs, used to rave about
him. He was a great matinee idol then, you know. Women used to
wait at the stage door just to see him come out. You can imagine how
excited I was when my father wrote me he and James Tyrone had
become friends, and that I was to meet him when I came home for
Easter vacation. I showed the letter to all the girls, and how envious
they were! My father took me to see him act first. It was a play about
the French Revolution and the leading part was a nobleman. I
couldn't take my eyes off him. I wept when he was thrown in prison
—and then was so mad at myself because I was afraid my eyes and
nose would be red. My father had said we'd go backstage to his
dressing room right after the play, and so we did.
>   *She gives a little excited, shy laugh.*
I was so bashful all I could do was stammer and blush like a little fool.
But he didn't seem to think I was a fool. I know he liked me the first
moment we were introduced.
>   *Coquettishly.*
I guess my eyes and nose couldn't have been red, after all. I was
really very pretty then, Cathleen. And he was handsomer than my
wildest dream, in his make-up and his nobleman's costume that was
so becoming to him. He was different from all ordinary men, like
someone from another world. At the same time he was simple, and
kind, and unassuming, not a bit stuck-up or vain. I fell in love right
then. So did he, he told me afterwards. I forgot all about becoming
a nun or a concert pianist. All I wanted was to be his wife.
>   *She pauses, staring before her with unnaturally bright,*
>   *dreamy eyes, and a rapt, tender, girlish smile.*
Thirty-six years ago, but I can see it as clearly as if it were tonight!
We've loved each other ever since. And in all those thirty-six years,
there has never been a breath of scandal about him. I mean, with any
other woman. Never since he met me. That has made me very happy,
Cathleen. It has made me forgive so many other things.

CATHLEEN
Fighting tipsy drowsiness—sentimentally.
He's a fine gentleman and you're a lucky woman.
Then, fidgeting.
Can I take the drink to Bridget, Ma'am? It must be near dinnertime
and I ought to be in the kitchen helping her. If she don't get some-
thing to quiet her temper, she'll be after me with the cleaver.

MARY
*With a vague exasperation at being brought back from her
dream.*
Yes, yes, go. I don't need you now.

CATHLEEN
With relief.
Thank you, Ma'am.
*She pours out a big drink and starts for the back parlor with
it.*
You won't be alone long. The Master and the boys—

MARY
Impatiently.
No, no, they won't come. Tell Bridget I won't wait. You can serve
dinner promptly at half past six. I'm not hungry but I'll sit at the
table and we'll get it over with.

CATHLEEN
You ought to eat something, Ma'am. It's a queer medicine if it takes
away your appetite.

MARY
Has begun to drift into dreams again—reacts mechanically.
What medicine? I don't know what you mean.
In dismissal.
You better take the drink to Bridget.

CATHLEEN
Yes, Ma'am.

*She disappears through the back parlor. Mary waits until
she hears the pantry door close behind her. Then she settles
back in relaxed dreaminess, staring fixedly at nothing. Her*

*arms rest limply along the arms of the chair, her hands with
long, warped, swollen-knuckled, sensitive fingers drooping
in complete calm. It is growing dark in the room. There is a
pause of dead quiet. Then from the world outside comes the
melancholy moan of the foghorn, followed by a chorus of
bells, muffled by the fog, from the anchored craft in the harbor. Mary's face gives no sign she has heard, but her hands
jerk and the fingers automatically play for a moment on the
air. She frowns and shakes her head mechanically as if a fly
had walked across her mind. She suddenly loses all the
girlish quality and is an aging, cynically sad, embittered
woman.*

MARY
Bitterly.

You're a sentimental fool. What is so wonderful about that first
meeting between a silly romantic schoolgirl and a matinee idol? You
were much happier before you knew he existed, in the Convent
when you used to pray to the Blessed Virgin.

Longingly.

If I could only find the faith I lost, so I could pray again!

*She pauses—then begins to recite the Hail Mary in a flat,
empty tone.*

"Hail, Mary, full of grace! The Lord is with Thee; blessed art Thou
among women."

Sneeringly.

You expect the Blessed Virgin to be fooled by a lying dope fiend
reciting words! You can't hide from her!

*She springs to her feet. Her hands fly up to pat her hair dis-
tractedly.*

I must go upstairs. I haven't taken enough. When you start again you
never know exactly how much you need.

*She goes toward the front parlor—then stops in the doorway
as she hears the sound of voices from the front path. She
starts guiltily.*

That must be them—

*She hurries back to sit down. Her face sets in stubborn de-
fensiveness—resentfully.*

Why are they coming back? They don't want to. And I'd much rather be alone.

> *Suddenly her whole manner changes. She becomes patheti-cally relieved and eager.*

Oh, I'm so glad they've come! I've been so horribly lonely!

> *The front door is heard closing and Tyrone calls uneasily from the hall.*

TYRONE

Are you there, Mary?

> *The light in the hall is turned on and shines through the front parlor to fall on Mary.*

MARY

> *Rises from her chair, her face lighting up lovingly—with excited eagerness.*

I'm here, dear. In the living room. I've been waiting for you.

> *Tyrone comes in through the front parlor. Edmund is behind him. Tyrone has had a lot to drink but beyond a slightly glazed look in his eyes and a trace of blur in his speech, he does not show it. Edmund has also had more than a few drinks without much apparent effect, except that his sunken cheeks are flushed and his eyes look bright and feverish. They stop in the doorway to stare appraisingly at her. What they see fulfills their worst expectations. But for the moment Mary is unconscious of their condemning eyes. She kisses her husband and then Edmund. Her manner is unnaturally effusive. They submit shrinkingly. She talks excitedly.*

I'm so happy you've come. I had given up hope. I was afraid you wouldn't come home. It's such a dismal, foggy evening. It must be much more cheerful in the barrooms uptown, where there are people you can talk and joke with. No, don't deny it. I know how you feel. I don't blame you a bit. I'm all the more grateful to you for coming home. I was sitting here so lonely and blue. Come and sit down.

> *She sits at left rear of table, Edmund at left of table, and Tyrone in the rocker at right of it.*

Dinner won't be ready for a minute. You're actually a little early. Will wonders never cease. Here's the whiskey, dear. Shall I pour a drink for you?

Without waiting for a reply she does so.

And you, Edmund? I don't want to encourage you, but one before dinner, as an appetizer, can't do any harm.

She pours a drink for him. They make no move to take the drinks. She talks on as if unaware of their silence.

Where's Jamie? But, of course, he'll never come home so long as he has the price of a drink left.

She reaches out and clasps her husband's hand—sadly.

I'm afraid Jamie has been lost to us for a long time, dear.

Her face hardens.

But we mustn't allow him to drag Edmund down with him, as he's like to do. He's jealous because Edmund has always been the baby— just as he used to be of Eugene. He'll never be content until he makes Edmund as hopeless a failure as he is.

EDMUND
Miserably.

Stop talking, Mama.

TYRONE
Dully.

Yes, Mary, the less you say now—

Then to Edmund, a bit tipsily.

All the same there's truth in your mother's warning. Beware of that brother of yours, or he'll poison life for you with his damned sneering serpent's tongue!

EDMUND
As before.

Oh, cut it out, Papa.

MARY
Goes on as if nothing had been said.

It's hard to believe, seeing Jamie as he is now, that he was ever my baby. Do you remember what a healthy, happy baby he was, James? The one-night stands and filthy trains and cheap hotels and bad food never made him cross or sick. He was always smiling or laughing. He hardly ever cried. Eugene was the same, too, happy and healthy, during the two years he lived before I let him die through my neglect.

TYRONE

Oh, for the love of God! I'm a fool for coming home!

EDMUND

Papa! Shut up!

MARY

Smiles with detached tenderness at Edmund.

It was Edmund who was the crosspatch when he was little, always getting upset and frightened about nothing at all.

She pats his hand—teasingly.

Everyone used to say, dear, you'd cry at the drop of a hat.

EDMUND

Cannot control his bitterness.

Maybe I guessed there was a good reason not to laugh.

TYRONE

Reproving and pitying.

Now, now, lad. You know better than to pay attention—

MARY

As if she hadn't heard—sadly again.

Who would have thought Jamie would grow up to disgrace us. You remember, James, for years after he went to boarding school, we received such glowing reports. Everyone liked him. All his teachers told us what a fine brain he had, and how easily he learned his lessons. Even after he began to drink and they had to expel him, they wrote us how sorry they were, because he was so likable and such a brilliant student. They predicted a wonderful future for him if he would only learn to take life seriously.

She pauses—then adds with a strange, sad detachment.

It's such a pity. Poor Jamie! It's hard to understand—

Abruptly a change comes over her. Her face hardens and she stares at her husband with accusing hostility.

No, it isn't at all. You brought him up to be a boozer. Since he first opened his eyes, he's seen you drinking. Always a bottle on the bureau in the cheap hotel rooms! And if he had a nightmare when he was little, or a stomach-ache, your remedy was to give him a teaspoonful of whiskey to quiet him.

TYRONE
Stung.

So I'm to blame because that lazy hulk has made a drunken loafer of himself? Is that what I came home to listen to? I might have known! When you have the poison in you, you want to blame everyone but yourself!

EDMUND

Papa! You told me not to pay attention.
Then, resentfully.
Anyway it's true. You did the same thing with me. I can remember that teaspoonful of booze every time I woke up with a nightmare.

MARY
In a detached reminiscent tone.

Yes, you were continually having nightmares as a child. You were born afraid. Because I was so afraid to bring you into the world.
She pauses—then goes on with the same detachment.
Please don't think I blame your father, Edmund. He didn't know any better. He never went to school after he was ten. His people were the most ignorant kind of poverty-stricken Irish. I'm sure they honestly believed whiskey is the healthiest medicine for a child who is sick or frightened.
Tyrone is about to burst out in angry defense of his family but Edmund intervenes.

EDMUND
Sharply.

Papa!
Changing the subject.
Are we going to have this drink, or aren't we?

TYRONE
Controlling himself—dully.

You're right. I'm a fool to take notice.
He picks up his glass listlessly.
Drink hearty, lad.

Edmund drinks but Tyrone remains staring at the glass in his hand. Edmund at once realizes how much the whiskey has been watered. He frowns, glancing from the bottle to his mother—starts to say something but stops.

MARY
In a changed tone—repentently.

I'm sorry if I sounded bitter, James. I'm not. It's all so far away. But I did feel a little hurt when you wished you hadn't come home. I was so relieved and happy when you came, and grateful to you. It's very dreary and sad to be here alone in the fog with night falling.

TYRONE
Moved.

I'm glad I came, Mary, when you act like your real self.

MARY

I was so lonesome I kept Cathleen with me just to have someone to talk to.

Her manner and quality drift back to the shy convent girl again.

Do you know what I was telling her, dear? About the night my father took me to your dressing room and I first fell in love with you. Do you remember?

TYRONE
Deeply moved—his voice husky.

Can you think I'd ever forget, Mary?

Edmund looks away from them, sad and embarrassed.

MARY
Tenderly.

No. I know you still love me, James, in spite of everything.

TYRONE
His face works and he blinks back tears—with quiet intensity.

Yes! As God is my judge! Always and forever, Mary!

MARY

And I love you, dear, in spite of everything.

There is a pause in which Edmund moves embarrassedly. The strange detachment comes over her manner again as if she were speaking impersonally of people seen from a distance.

But I must confess, James, although I couldn't help loving you, I would never have married you if I'd known you drank so much. I remember the first night your barroom friends had to help you up to the door of our hotel room, and knocked and then ran away before I came to the door. We were still on our honeymoon, do you remember?

TYRONE
With guilty vehemence.

I don't remember! It wasn't on our honeymoon! And I never in my life had to be helped to bed, or missed a performance!

MARY
As though he hadn't spoken.

I had waited in that ugly hotel room hour after hour. I kept making excuses for you. I told myself it must be some business connected with the theater. I knew so little about the theater. Then I became terrified. I imagined all sorts of horrible accidents. I got on my knees and prayed that nothing had happened to you—and then they brought you up and left you outside the door.

She gives a little, sad sigh.

I didn't know how often that was to happen in the years to come, how many times I was to wait in ugly hotel rooms. I became quite used to it.

EDMUND
Bursts out with a look of accusing hate at his father.

Christ! No wonder— !

He controls himself—gruffly.

When is dinner, Mama? It must be time.

TYRONE
Overwhelmed by shame which he tries to hide, fumbles with his watch.

Yes. It must be. Let's see.

He stares at his watch without seeing it. Pleadingly.

Mary! Can't you forget—?

MARY

With detached pity.

No, dear. But I forgive. I always forgive you. So don't look so guilty. I'm sorry I remembered out loud. I don't want to be sad, or to make you sad. I want to remember only the happy part of the past.

Her manner drifts back to the shy, gay convent girl.

Do you remember our wedding, dear? I'm sure you've completely forgotten what my wedding gown looked like. Men don't notice such things. They don't think they're important. But it was important to me, I can tell you! How I fussed and worried! I was so excited and happy! My father told me to buy anything I wanted and never mind what it cost. The best is none too good, he said. I'm afraid he spoiled me dreadfully. My mother didn't. She was very pious and strict. I think she was a little jealous. She didn't approve of my marrying—especially an actor. I think she hoped I would become a nun. She used to scold my father. She'd grumble, "You never tell me, never mind what it costs, when I buy anything! You've spoiled that girl so, I pity her husband if she ever marries. She'll expect him to give her the moon. She'll never make a good wife."

She laughs affectionately.

Poor mother!

She smiles at Tyrone with a strange, incongruous coquetry.

But she was mistaken, wasn't she, James? I haven't been such a bad wife, have I?

TYRONE

Huskily, trying to force a smile.

I'm not complaining, Mary.

MARY

A shadow of vague guilt crosses her face.

At least, I've loved you dearly, and done the best I could—under the circumstances.

The shadow vanishes and her shy, girlish expression returns.

That wedding gown was nearly the death of me and the dressmaker, too!

She laughs.

I was so particular. It was never quite good enough. At last she said she refused to touch it any more or she might spoil it, and I made her leave so I could be alone to examine myself in the mirror. I was so pleased and vain. I thought to myself, "Even if your nose and mouth and ears are a trifle too large, your eyes and hair and figure, and your hands, make up for it. You're just as pretty as any actress he's ever met, and you don't have to use paint."

She pauses, wrinkling her brow in an effort of memory.

Where is my wedding gown now, I wonder? I kept it wrapped up in tissue paper in my trunk. I used to hope I would have a daughter and when it came time for her to marry— She couldn't have bought a lovelier gown, and I knew, James, you'd never tell her, never mind the cost. You'd want her to pick up something at a bargain. It was made of soft, shimmering satin, trimmed with wonderful old duchesse lace, in tiny ruffles around the neck and sleeves, and worked in with the folds that were draped round in a bustle effect at the back. The basque was boned and very tight. I remember I held my breath when it was fitted, so my waist would be as small as possible. My father even let me have duchesse lace on my white satin slippers, and lace with the orange blossoms in my veil. Oh, how I loved that gown! It was so beautiful! Where is it now, I wonder? I used to take it out from time to time when I was lonely, but it always made me cry, so finally a long while ago—

She wrinkles her forehead again.

I wonder where I hid it? Probably in one of the old trunks in the attic. Some day I'll have to look.

She stops, staring before her. Tyrone sighs, shaking his head hopelessly, and attempts to catch his son's eye, looking for sympathy, but Edmund is staring at the floor.

TYRONE
Forces a casual tone.

Isn't it dinner time, dear?

With a feeble attempt at teasing.

You're forever scolding me for being late, but now I'm on time for once, it's dinner that's late.

She doesn't appear to hear him. He adds, still pleasantly.

Well, if I can't eat yet, I can drink. I'd forgotten I had this.

*He drinks his drink. Edmund watches him. Tyrone scowls
and looks at his wife with sharp suspicion—roughly.*

Who's been tampering with my whiskey? The damned stuff is half
water! Jamie's been away and he wouldn't overdo his trick like this,
anyway. Any fool could tell— Mary, answer me!

With angry disgust.

I hope to God you haven't taken to drink on top of—

EDMUND

Shut up, Papa!

To his mother, without looking at her.

You treated Cathleen and Bridget, isn't that it, Mama?

MARY

With indifferent casualness.

Yes, of course. They work hard for poor wages. And I'm the house-
keeper, I have to keep them from leaving. Besides, I wanted to treat
Cathleen because I had her drive uptown with me, and sent her to
get my prescription filled.

EDMUND

For God's sake, Mama! You can't trust her! Do you want everyone
on earth to know?

MARY

Her face hardening stubbornly.

Know what? That I suffer from rheumatism in my hands and have
to take medicine to kill the pain? Why should I be ashamed of that?

*Turns on Edmund with a hard, accusing antagonism—al-
most a revengeful enmity.*

I never knew what rheumatism was before you were born! Ask your
father!

Edmund looks away, shrinking into himself.

TYRONE

Don't mind her, lad. It doesn't mean anything. When she gets to the
stage where she gives the old crazy excuse about her hands she's gone
far away from us.

MARY

Turns on him—with a strangely triumphant, taunting smile.

I'm glad you realize that, James! Now perhaps you'll give up trying to remind me, you and Edmund!

> *Abruptly, in a detached, matter-of-fact tone.*

Why don't you light the light, James? It's getting dark. I know you hate to, but Edmund has proved to you that one bulb burning doesn't cost much. There's no sense letting your fear of the poorhouse make you too stingy.

TYRONE
> *Reacts mechanically.*

I never claimed one bulb cost much! It's having them on, one here and one there, that makes the Electric Light Company rich.

> *He gets up and turns on the reading lamp—roughly.*

But I'm a fool to talk reason to you.

> *To Edmund.*

I'll get a fresh bottle of whiskey, lad, and we'll have a real drink.

> *He goes through the back parlor.*

MARY
> *With detached amusement.*

He'll sneak around to the outside cellar door so the servants won't see him. He's really ashamed of keeping his whiskey padlocked in the cellar. Your father is a strange man, Edmund. It took many years before I understood him. You must try to understand and forgive him, too, and not feel contempt because he's close-fisted. His father deserted his mother and their six children a year or so after they came to America. He told them he had a premonition he would die soon, and he was homesick for Ireland, and wanted to go back there to die. So he went and he did die. He must have been a peculiar man, too. Your father had to go to work in a machine shop when he was only ten years old.

EDMUND
> *Protests dully.*

Oh, for Pete's sake, Mama. I've heard Papa tell that machine shop story ten thousand times.

MARY

Yes, dear, you've had to listen, but I don't think you've ever tried to understand.

EDMUND
Ignoring this—miserably.
Listen, Mama! You're not so far gone yet you've forgotten everything. You haven't asked me what I found out this afternoon. Don't
you care a damn?

MARY
Shakenly.
Don't say that! You hurt me, dear!

EDMUND
What I've got is serious, Mama. Doc Hardy knows for sure now.

MARY
Stiffens into scornful, defensive stubbornness.
That lying old quack! I warned you he'd invent— !

EDMUND
Miserably dogged.
He called in a specialist to examine me, so he'd be absolutely sure.

MARY
Ignoring this.
Don't tell me about Hardy! If you heard what the doctor at the sanatorium, who really knows something, said about how he'd treated
me! He said he ought to be locked up! He said it was a wonder I
hadn't gone mad! I told him I had once, that time I ran down in my
nightdress to throw myself off the dock. You remember that, don't
you? And yet you want me to pay attention to what Doctor Hardy
says. Oh, no!

EDMUND
Bitterly.
I remember, all right. It was right after that Papa and Jamie decided
they couldn't hide it from me any more. Jamie told me. I called him
a liar! I tried to punch him in the nose. But I knew he wasn't lying.
His voice trembles, his eyes begin to fill with tears.
God, it made everything in life seem rotten!

MARY
Pitiably.
Oh, don't. My baby! You hurt me so dreadfully!

EDMUND
Dully.

I'm sorry, Mama. It was you who brought it up.

Then with a bitter, stubborn persistence.

Listen, Mama. I'm going to tell you whether you want to hear or not. I've got to go to a sanatorium.

MARY
Dazedly, as if this was something that had never occurred to her.

Go away?

Violently.

No! I won't have it! How dare Doctor Hardy advise such a thing without consulting me! How dare your father allow him! What right has he? You are my baby! Let him attend to Jamie!

More and more excited and bitter.

I know why he wants you sent to a sanatorium. To take you from me! He's always tried to do that. He's been jealous of every one of my babies! He kept finding ways to make me leave them. That's what caused Eugene's death. He's been jealous of you most of all. He knew I loved you most because—

EDMUND
Miserably.

Oh, stop talking crazy, can't you, Mama! Stop trying to blame him. And why are you so against my going away now? I've been away a lot, and I've never noticed it broke your heart!

MARY
Bitterly.

I'm afraid you're not very sensitive, after all.

Sadly.

You might have guessed, dear, that after I knew you knew—about me—I had to be glad whenever you were where you couldn't see me.

EDMUND
Brokenly.

Mama! Don't!

He reaches out blindly and takes her hand—but he drops it immediately, overcome by bitterness again.

All this talk about loving me—and you won't even listen when I try to tell you how sick—

MARY

With an abrupt transformation into a detached bullying motherliness.

Now, now. That's enough! I don't care to hear because I know it's nothing but Hardy's ignorant lies.

He shrinks back into himself. She keeps on in a forced, teasing tone but with an increasing undercurrent of resentment.

You're so like your father, dear. You love to make a scene out of nothing so you can be dramatic and tragic.

With a belittling laugh.

If I gave you the slightest encouragement, you'd tell me next you were going to die—

EDMUND

People do die of it. Your own father—

MARY

Sharply.

Why do you mention him? There's no comparison at all with you. He had consumption.

Angrily.

I hate you when you become gloomy and morbid! I forbid you to remind me of my father's death, do you hear me?

EDMUND

His face hard—grimly.

Yes, I hear you, Mama. I wish to God I didn't!

He gets up from his chair and stands staring condemningly at her—bitterly.

It's pretty hard to take at times, having a dope fiend for a mother!

She winces—all life seeming to drain from her face, leaving it with the appearance of a plaster cast. Instantly Edmund wishes he could take back what he has said. He stammers miserably.

Forgive me, Mama. I was angry. You hurt me.

There is a pause in which the foghorn and the ships' bells are heard.

120

MARY

Goes slowly to the windows at right like an automaton—looking out, a blank, far-off quality in her voice.

Just listen to that awful foghorn. And the bells. Why is it fog makes everything sound so sad and lost, I wonder?

EDMUND

Brokenly.

I—I can't stay here. I don't want any dinner.

He hurries away through the front parlor. She keeps staring out the window until she hears the front door close behind him. Then she comes back and sits in her chair, the same blank look on her face.

MARY

Vaguely.

I must go upstairs. I haven't taken enough.

She pauses—then longingly.

I hope, sometime, without meaning it, I will take an overdose. I never could do it deliberately. The Blessed Virgin would never forgive me, then.

She hears Tyrone returning and turns as he comes in, through the back parlor, with a bottle of whiskey he has just uncorked. He is fuming.

TYRONE

Wrathfully.

The padlock is all scratched. That drunken loafer has tried to pick the lock with a piece of wire, the way he's done before.

With satisfaction, as if this was a perpetual battle of wits with his elder son.

But I've fooled him this time. It's a special padlock a professional burglar couldn't pick.

He puts the bottle on the tray and suddenly is aware of Edmund's absence.

Where's Edmund?

MARY

With a vague far-away air.

He went out. Perhaps he's going uptown again to find Jamie. He still has some money left, I suppose, and it's burning a hole in his pocket. He said he didn't want any dinner. He doesn't seem to have any appetite these days.

> *Then stubbornly.*

But it's just a summer cold.

> *Tyrone stares at her and shakes his head helplessly and pours himself a big drink and drinks it. Suddenly it is too much for her and she breaks out and sobs.*

Oh, James, I'm so frightened!

> *She gets up and throws her arms around him and hides her face on his shoulder—sobbingly.*

I know he's going to die!

TYRONE

Don't say that! It's not true! They promised me in six months he'd be cured.

MARY

You don't believe that! I can tell when you're acting! And it will be my fault. I should never have borne him. It would have been better for his sake. I could never hurt him then. He wouldn't have had to know his mother was a dope fiend—and hate her!

TYRONE

> *His voice quivering.*

Hush, Mary, for the love of God! He loves you. He knows it was a curse put on you without your knowing or willing it. He's proud you're his mother!

> *Abruptly as he hears the pantry door opening.*

Hush, now! Here comes Cathleen. You don't want her to see you crying.

> *She turns quickly away from him to the windows at right, hastily wiping her eyes. A moment later Cathleen appears in the back-parlor doorway. She is uncertain in her walk and grinning woozily.*

CATHLEEN

> *Starts guiltily when she sees Tyrone—with dignity.*

Dinner is served, Sir.

> *Raising her voice unnecessarily.*

Dinner is served, Ma'am.

She forgets her dignity and addresses Tyrone with good-natured familiarity.

So you're here, are you? Well, well. Won't Bridget be in a rage! I told her the Madame said you wouldn't be home.

Then reading accusation in his eye.

Don't be looking at me that way. If I've a drop taken, I didn't steal it. I was invited.

She turns with huffy dignity and disappears through the back parlor.

TYRONE

Sighs—then summoning his actor's heartiness.

Come along, dear. Let's have our dinner. I'm hungry as a hunter.

MARY

Comes to him—her face is composed in plaster again and her tone is remote.

I'm afraid you'll have to excuse me, James. I couldn't possibly eat anything. My hands pain me dreadfully. I think the best thing for me is to go to bed and rest. Good night, dear.

She kisses him mechanically and turns toward the front parlor.

TYRONE

Harshly.

Up to take more of that God-damned poison, is that it? You'll be like a mad ghost before the night's over!

MARY

Starts to walk away—blankly.

I don't know what you're talking about, James. You say such mean, bitter things when you've drunk too much. You're as bad as Jamie or Edmund.

She moves off through the front parlor. He stands a second as if not knowing what to do. He is a sad, bewildered, broken old man. He walks wearily off through the back parlor toward the dining room.

CURTAIN

Act Four

SCENE   *The same. It is around midnight. The lamp in the front hall has been turned out, so that now no light shines through the front parlor. In the living room only the reading lamp on the table is lighted. Outside the windows the wall of fog appears denser than ever. As the curtain rises, the foghorn is heard, followed by the ships' bells from the harbor.*

Tyrone is seated at the table. He wears his pince-nez, and is playing solitaire. He has taken off his coat and has on an old brown dressing gown. The whiskey bottle on the tray is three-quarters empty. There is a fresh full bottle on the table, which he has brought from the cellar so there will be an ample reserve at hand. He is drunk and shows it by the owlish, deliberate manner in which he peers at each card to make certain of its identity, and then plays it as if he wasn't certain of his aim. His eyes have a misted, oily look and his mouth is slack. But despite all the whiskey in him, he has not escaped, and he looks as he appeared at the close of the preceding act, a sad, defeated old man, possessed by hopeless resignation.

As the curtain rises, he finishes a game and sweeps the cards together. He shuffles them clumsily, dropping a couple on the floor. He retrieves them with difficulty, and starts to shuffle again, when he hears someone entering the front door. He peers over his pince-nez through the front parlor.

TYRONE
His voice thick.
Who's that? Is it you, Edmund?
Edmund's voice answers curtly, "Yes." Then he evidently collides with something in the dark hall and can be heard cursing. A moment later the hall lamp is turned on. Tyrone frowns and calls.

Turn that light out before you come in.

But Edmund doesn't. He comes in through the front parlor.
He is drunk now, too, but like his father he carries it well,
and gives little physical sign of it except in his eyes and a
chip-on-the-shoulder aggressiveness in his manner. Tyrone
speaks, at first with a warm, relieved welcome.

I'm glad you've come, lad. I've been damned lonely.

Then resentfully.

You're a fine one to run away and leave me to sit alone here all night
when you know—

With sharp irritation.

I told you to turn out that light! We're not giving a ball. There's no
reason to have the house ablaze with electricity at this time of night,
burning up money!

EDMUND

Angrily.

Ablaze with electricity! One bulb! Hell, everyone keeps a light on
in the front hall until they go to bed.

He rubs his knee.

I damned near busted my knee on the hat stand.

TYRONE

The light from here shows in the hall. You could see your way well
enough if you were sober.

EDMUND

If *I* was sober? I like that!

TYRONE

I don't give a damn what other people do. If they want to be waste-
ful fools, for the sake of show, let them be!

EDMUND

One bulb! Christ, don't be such a cheap skate! I've proved by figures
if you left the light bulb on all night it wouldn't be as much as one
drink!

TYRONE

To hell with your figures! The proof is in the bills I have to pay!

EDMUND

Sits down opposite his father—contemptuously.

Yes, facts don't mean a thing, do they? What you want to believe, that's the only truth!

Derisively.

Shakespeare was an Irish Catholic, for example.

TYRONE

Stubbornly.

So he was. The proof is in his plays.

EDMUND

Well he wasn't, and there's no proof of it in his plays, except to you!

Jeeringly.

The Duke of Wellington, there was another good Irish Catholic!

TYRONE

I never said he was a good one. He was a renegade but a Catholic just the same.

EDMUND

Well, he wasn't. You just want to believe no one but an Irish Catholic general could beat Napoleon.

TYRONE

I'm not going to argue with you. I asked you to turn out that light in the hall.

EDMUND

I heard you, and as far as I'm concerned it stays on.

TYRONE

None of your damned insolence! Are you going to obey me or not?

EDMUND

Not! If you want to be a crazy miser put it out yourself!

TYRONE

With threatening anger.

Listen to me! I've put up with a lot from you because from the mad things you've done at times I've thought you weren't quite right in your head. I've excused you and never lifted my hand to you. But there's a straw that breaks the camel's back. You'll obey me and put out that light or, big as you are, I'll give you a thrashing that'll teach you— !

Suddenly he remembers Edmund's illness and instantly becomes guilty and shamefaced.

Forgive me, lad. I forgot— You shouldn't goad me into losing my temper.

EDMUND
Ashamed himself now.

Forget it, Papa. I apologize, too. I had no right being nasty about nothing. I am a bit soused, I guess. I'll put out the damned light.

He starts to get up.

TYRONE

No, stay where you are. Let it burn.

He stands up abruptly—and a bit drunkenly—and begins turning on the three bulbs in the chandelier, with a childish, bitterly dramatic self-pity.

We'll have them all on! Let them burn! To hell with them! The poorhouse is the end of the road, and it might as well be sooner as later!

He finishes turning on the lights.

EDMUND
Has watched this proceeding with an awakened sense of humor—now he grins, teasing affectionately.

That's a grand curtain.

He laughs.

You're a wonder, Papa.

TYRONE
Sits down sheepishly—grumbles pathetically.

That's right, laugh at the old fool! The poor old ham! But the final curtain will be in the poorhouse just the same, and that's not comedy!

Then as Edmund is still grinning, he changes the subject.

Well, well, let's not argue. You've got brains in that head of yours, though you do your best to deny them. You'll live to learn the value of a dollar. You're not like your damned tramp of a brother. I've given up hope he'll ever get sense. Where is he, by the way?

EDMUND

How would I know?

TYRONE

I thought you'd gone back uptown to meet him.

EDMUND

No. I walked out to the beach. I haven't seen him since this afternoon.

TYRONE

Well, if you split the money I gave you with him, like a fool—

EDMUND

Sure I did. He's always staked me when he had anything.

TYRONE

Then it doesn't take a soothsayer to tell he's probably in the whore-house.

EDMUND

What of it if he is? Why not?

TYRONE

Contemptuously.

Why not, indeed. It's the fit place for him. If he's ever had a loftier dream than whores and whiskey, he's never shown it.

EDMUND

Oh, for Pete's sake, Papa! If you're going to start that stuff, I'll beat it.

He starts to get up.

TYRONE

Placatingly.

All right, all right, I'll stop. God knows, I don't like the subject either. Will you join me in a drink?

EDMUND

Ah! Now you're talking!

TYRONE

Passes the bottle to him—mechanically.

I'm wrong to treat you. You've had enough already.

EDMUND

Pouring a big drink—a bit drunkenly.

Enough is *not* as good as a feast.
He hands back the bottle.

TYRONE

It's too much in your condition.

EDMUND

Forget my condition!
He raises his glass.
Here's how.

TYRONE

Drink hearty.
They drink.
If you walked all the way to the beach you must be damp and chilled.

EDMUND

Oh, I dropped in at the Inn on the way out and back.

TYRONE

It's not a night I'd pick for a long walk.

EDMUND

I loved the fog. It was what I needed.
He sounds more tipsy and looks it.

TYRONE

You should have more sense than to risk—

EDMUND

To hell with sense! We're all crazy. What do we want with sense?
He quotes from Dowson sardonically.
  "They are not long, the weeping and the laughter,
  Love and desire and hate:
  I think they have no portion in us after
  We pass the gate.

  They are not long, the days of wine and roses:
  Out of a misty dream
  Our path emerges for a while, then closes
  Within a dream."

Staring before him.

The fog was where I wanted to be. Halfway down the path you can't see this house. You'd never know it was here. Or any of the other places down the avenue. I couldn't see but a few feet ahead. I didn't meet a soul. Everything looked and sounded unreal. Nothing was what it is. That's what I wanted—to be alone with myself in another world where truth is untrue and life can hide from itself. Out beyond the harbor, where the road runs along the beach, I even lost the feeling of being on land. The fog and the sea seemed part of each other. It was like walking on the bottom of the sea. As if I had drowned long ago. As if I was a ghost belonging to the fog, and the fog was the ghost of the sea. It felt damned peaceful to be nothing more than a ghost within a ghost.

He sees his father staring at him with mingled worry and irritated disapproval. He grins mockingly.

Don't look at me as if I'd gone nutty. I'm talking sense. Who wants to see life as it is, if they can help it? It's the three Gorgons in one. You look in their faces and turn to stone. Or it's Pan. You see him and you die—that is, inside you—and have to go on living as a ghost.

TYRONE

Impressed and at the same time revolted.

You have a poet in you but it's a damned morbid one!

Forcing a smile.

Devil take your pessimism. I feel low-spirited enough.

He sighs.

Why can't you remember your Shakespeare and forget the third-raters. You'll find what you're trying to say in him—as you'll find everything else worth saying.

He quotes, using his fine voice.

"We are such stuff as dreams are made on, and our little life is rounded with a sleep."

EDMUND

Ironically.

Fine! That's beautiful. But I wasn't trying to say that. We are such stuff as manure is made on, so let's drink up and forget it. That's more my idea.

TYRONE
Disgustedly.

Ach! Keep such sentiments to yourself. I shouldn't have given you that drink.

EDMUND

It did pack a wallop, all right. On you, too.
He grins with affectionate teasing.
Even if you've never missed a performance!
Aggressively.
Well, what's wrong with being drunk? It's what we're after, isn't it? Let's not kid each other, Papa. Not tonight. We know what we're trying to forget.
Hurriedly.
But let's not talk about it. It's no use now.

TYRONE
Dully.
No. All we can do is try to be resigned—again.

EDMUND

Or be so drunk you can forget.
He recites, and recites well, with bitter, ironical passion, the Symons' translation of Baudelaire's prose poem.
"Be always drunken. Nothing else matters: that is the only question. If you would not feel the horrible burden of Time weighing on your shoulders and crushing you to the earth, be drunken continually.

Drunken with what? With wine, with poetry, or with virtue, as you will. But be drunken.

And if sometimes, on the stairs of a palace, or on the green side of a ditch, or in the dreary solitude of your own room, you should awaken and the drunkenness be half or wholly slipped away from you, ask of the wind, or of the wave, or of the star, or of the bird, or of the clock, of whatever flies, or sighs, or rocks, or sings, or speaks, ask what hour it is; and the wind, wave, star, bird, clock, will answer you: 'It is the hour to be drunken! Be drunken, if you would not be martyred slaves of Time; be drunken continually! With wine, with poetry, or with virtue, as you will.' "
He grins at his father provocatively.

TYRONE
Thickly humorous.

I wouldn't worry about the virtue part of it, if I were you.
Then disgustedly.

Pah! It's morbid nonsense! What little truth is in it you'll find nobly said in Shakespeare.
Then appreciatively.

But you recited it well, lad. Who wrote it?

EDMUND
Baudelaire.

TYRONE
Never heard of him.

EDMUND
Grins provocatively.

He also wrote a poem about Jamie and the Great White Way.

TYRONE
That loafer! I hope to God he misses the last car and has to stay up-town!

EDMUND
Goes on, ignoring this.

Although he was French and never saw Broadway and died before Jamie was born. He knew him and Little Old New York just the same.
He recites the Symons' translation of Baudelaire's "Epilogue."

"With heart at rest I climbed the citadel's
Steep height, and saw the city as from a tower,
Hospital, brothel, prison, and such hells,

Where evil comes up softly like a flower.
Thou knowest, O Satan, patron of my pain,
Not for vain tears I went up at that hour;

But like an old sad faithful lecher, fain
To drink delight of that enormous trull
Whose hellish beauty makes me young again.

Whether thou sleep, with heavy vapours full,
Sodden with day, or, new apparelled, stand
In gold-laced veils of evening beautiful,

I love thee, infamous city! Harlots and
Hunted have pleasures of their own to give,
The vulgar herd can never understand."

TYRONE
With irritable disgust.

Morbid filth! Where the hell do you get your taste in literature?
Filth and despair and pessimism! Another atheist, I suppose. When
you deny God, you deny hope. That's the trouble with you. If you'd
get down on your knees—

EDMUND
As if he hadn't heard—sardonically.

It's a good likeness of Jamie, don't you think, hunted by himself and
whiskey, hiding in a Broadway hotel room with some fat tart—he
likes them fat—reciting Dowson's Cynara to her.

He recites derisively, but with deep feeling.

"All night upon mine heart I felt her warm heart beat,
Night-long within mine arms in love and sleep she lay;
Surely the kisses of her bought red mouth were sweet;
But I was desolate and sick of an old passion,
When I awoke and found the dawn was gray:
I have been faithful to thee, Cynara! in my fashion."

Jeeringly.

And the poor fat burlesque queen doesn't get a word of it, but sus-
pects she's being insulted! And Jamie never loved any Cynara, and
was never faithful to a woman in his life, even in his fashion! But he
lies there, kidding himself he is superior and enjoys pleasures "the
vulgar herd can never understand"!

He laughs.

It's nuts—completely nuts!

TYRONE
Vaguely—his voice thick.

It's madness, yes. If you'd get on your knees and pray. When you
deny God, you deny sanity.

EDMUND
Ignoring this.

But who am I to feel superior? I've done the same damned thing.
And it's no more crazy than Dowson himself, inspired by an absinthe
hangover, writing it to a dumb barmaid, who thought he was a poor
crazy souse, and gave him the gate to marry a waiter!

He laughs—then soberly, with genuine sympathy.

Poor Dowson. Booze and consumption got him.

*He starts and for a second looks miserable and frightened.
Then with defensive irony.*

Perhaps it would be tactful of me to change the subject.

TYRONE
Thickly.

Where you get your taste in authors— That damned library of yours!

He indicates the small bookcase at rear.

Voltaire, Rousseau, Schopenhauer, Nietzsche, Ibsen! Atheists, fools,
and madmen! And your poets! This Dowson, and this Baudelaire,
and Swinburne and Oscar Wilde, and Whitman and Poe! Whore-
mongers and degenerates! Pah! When I've three good sets of Shakespeare there (*he nods at the large bookcase*) you could read.

EDMUND
Provocatively.

They say he was a souse, too.

TYRONE

They lie! I don't doubt he liked his glass—it's a good man's failing—
but he knew how to drink so it didn't poison his brain with morbidness and filth. Don't compare him with the pack you've got in
there.

He indicates the small bookcase again.

Your dirty Zola! And your Dante Gabriel Rossetti who was a dope
fiend!

He starts and looks guilty.

EDMUND
With defensive dryness.

Perhaps it would be wise to change the subject.

A pause.

You can't accuse me of not knowing Shakespeare. Didn't I win five dollars from you once when you bet me I couldn't learn a leading part of his in a week, as you used to do in stock in the old days. I learned Macbeth and recited it letter perfect, with you giving me the cues.

> TYRONE
> *Approvingly.*

That's true. So you did.

> *He smiles teasingly and sighs.*

It was a terrible ordeal, I remember, hearing you murder the lines. I kept wishing I'd paid over the bet without making you prove it.

> *He chuckles and Edmund grins. Then he starts as he hears a sound from upstairs—with dread.*

Did you hear? She's moving around. I was hoping she'd gone to sleep.

> EDMUND

Forget it! How about another drink?

> *He reaches out and gets the bottle, pours a drink and hands it back. Then with a strained casualness, as his father pours a drink.*

When did Mama go to bed?

> TYRONE

Right after you left. She wouldn't eat any dinner. What made you run away?

> EDMUND

Nothing.

> *Abruptly raising his glass.*

Well, here's how.

> TYRONE
> *Mechanically.*

Drink hearty, lad.

> *They drink. Tyrone again listens to sounds upstairs—with dread.*

She's moving around a lot. I hope to God she doesn't come down.

EDMUND
Dully.

Yes. She'll be nothing but a ghost haunting the past by this time.
He pauses—then miserably.

Back before I was born—

TYRONE

Doesn't she do the same with me? Back before she ever knew me.
You'd think the only happy days she's ever known were in her
father's home, or at the Convent, praying and playing the piano.
Jealous resentment in his bitterness.

As I've told you before, you must take her memories with a grain
of salt. Her wonderful home was ordinary enough. Her father
wasn't the great, generous, noble Irish gentleman she makes out. He
was a nice enough man, good company and a good talker. I liked
him and he liked me. He was prosperous enough, too, in his whole-
sale grocery business, an able man. But he had his weakness. She con-
demns my drinking but she forgets his. It's true he never touched a
drop till he was forty, but after that he made up for lost time. He
became a steady champagne drinker, the worst kind. That was his
grand pose, to drink only champagne. Well, it finished him quick—
that and the consumption—
He stops with a guilty glance at his son.

EDMUND
Sardonically.

We don't seem able to avoid unpleasant topics, do we?

TYRONE
Sighs sadly.

No.
Then with a pathetic attempt at heartiness.

What do you say to a game or two of Casino, lad?

EDMUND

All right.

TYRONE
Shuffling the cards clumsily.

We can't lock up and go to bed till Jamie comes on the last trolley—

which I hope he won't—and I don't want to go upstairs, anyway, till she's asleep.

EDMUND

Neither do I.

TYRONE

Keeps shuffling the cards fumblingly, forgetting to deal them.
As I was saying, you must take her tales of the past with a grain of salt. The piano playing and her dream of becoming a concert pianist. That was put in her head by the nuns flattering her. She was their pet. They loved her for being so devout. They're innocent women, anyway, when it comes to the world. They don't know that not one in a million who shows promise ever rises to concert playing. Not that your mother didn't play well for a schoolgirl, but that's no reason to take it for granted she could have—

EDMUND

Sharply.
Why don't you deal, if we're going to play.

TYRONE

Eh? I am.

Dealing with very uncertain judgment of distance.
And the idea she might have become a nun. That's the worst. Your mother was one of the most beautiful girls you could ever see. She knew it, too. She was a bit of a rogue and a coquette, God bless her, behind all her shyness and blushes. She was never made to renounce the world. She was bursting with health and high spirits and the love of loving.

EDMUND

For God's sake, Papa! Why don't you pick up your hand?

TYRONE

Picks it up—dully.
Yes, let's see what I have here.

They both stare at their cards unseeingly. Then they both start. Tyrone whispers.

Listen!

EDMUND
She's coming downstairs.

TYRONE
Hurriedly.
We'll play our game. Pretend not to notice and she'll soon go up again.

EDMUND
Staring through the front parlor—with relief.
I don't see her. She must have started down and then turned back.

TYRONE
Thank God.

EDMUND
Yes. It's pretty horrible to see her the way she must be now.
With bitter misery.
The hardest thing to take is the blank wall she builds around her. Or it's more like a bank of fog in which she hides and loses herself. Deliberately, that's the hell of it! You know something in her does it deliberately—to get beyond our reach, to be rid of us, to forget we're alive! It's as if, in spite of loving us, she hated us!

TYRONE
Remonstrates gently.
Now, now, lad. It's not her. It's the damned poison.

EDMUND
Bitterly.
She takes it to get that effect. At least, I know she did this time!
Abruptly.
My play, isn't it? Here.
He plays a card.

TYRONE
Plays mechanically—gently reproachful.
She's been terriby frightened about your illness, for all her pretending. Don't be too hard on her, lad. Remember she's not responsible. Once that cursed poison gets a hold on anyone—

EDMUND

His face grows hard and he stares at his father with bitter accusation.

It never should have gotten a hold on her! I know damned well she's not to blame! And I know who is! You are! Your damned stinginess! If you'd spent money for a decent doctor when she was so sick after I was born, she'd never have known morphine existed! Instead you put her in the hands of a hotel quack who wouldn't admit his ignorance and took the easiest way out, not giving a damn what happened to her afterwards! All because his fee was cheap! Another one of your bargains!

TYRONE

Stung—angrily.

Be quiet! How dare you talk of something you know nothing about!

Trying to control his temper.

You must try to see my side of it, too, lad. How was I to know he was that kind of a doctor? He had a good reputation—

EDMUND

Among the souses in the hotel bar, I suppose!

TYRONE

That's a lie! I asked the hotel proprietor to recommend the best—

EDMUND

Yes! At the same time crying poorhouse and making it plain you wanted a cheap one! I know your system! By God, I ought to after this afternoon!

TYRONE

Guiltily defensive.

What about this afternoon?

EDMUND

Never mind now. We're talking about Mama! I'm saying no matter how you excuse yourself you know damned well your stinginess is to blame—

TYRONE

And I say you're a liar! Shut your mouth right now, or—

EDMUND
Ignoring this.

After you found out she'd been made a morphine addict, why didn't you send her to a cure then, at the start, while she still had a chance? No, that would have meant spending some money! I'll bet you told her all she had to do was use a little will power! That's what you still believe in your heart, in spite of what doctors, who really know something about it, have told you!

TYRONE

You lie again! I know better than that now! But how was I to know then? What did I know of morphine? It was years before I discovered what was wrong. I thought she'd never got over her sickness, that's all. Why didn't I send her to a cure, you say?

Bitterly.

Haven't I? I've spent thousands upon thousands in cures! A waste. What good have they done her? She always started again.

EDMUND

Because you've never given her anything that would help her want to stay off it! No home except this summer dump in a place she hates and you've refused even to spend money to make this look decent, while you keep buying more property, and playing sucker for every con man with a gold mine, or a silver mine, or any kind of get-rich-quick swindle! You've dragged her around on the road, season after season, on one-night stands, with no one she could talk to, waiting night after night in dirty hotel rooms for you to come back with a bun on after the bars closed! Christ, is it any wonder she didn't want to be cured. Jesus, when I think of it I hate your guts!

TYRONE
Strickenly.

Edmund!
Then in a rage.

How dare you talk to your father like that, you insolent young cub! After all I've done for you.

EDMUND

We'll come to that, what you're doing for me!

TYRONE

Looking guilty again—ignores this.

Will you stop repeating your mother's crazy accusations, which she never makes unless it's the poison talking? I never dragged her on the road against her will. Naturally, I wanted her with me. I loved her. And she came because she loved me and wanted to be with me. That's the truth, no matter what she says when she's not herself. And she needn't have been lonely. There was always the members of my company to talk to, if she'd wanted. She had her children, too, and I insisted, in spite of the expense, on having a nurse to travel with her.

EDMUND

Bitterly.

Yes, your one generosity, and that because you were jealous of her paying too much attention to us, and wanted us out of your way! It was another mistake, too! If she'd had to take care of me all by herself, and had that to occupy her mind, maybe she'd have been able—

TYRONE

Goaded into vindictiveness.

Or for that matter, if you insist on judging things by what she says when she's not in her right mind, if you hadn't been born she'd never—

He stops ashamed.

EDMUND

Suddenly spent and miserable.

Sure. I know that's what she feels, Papa.

TYRONE

Protests penitently.

She doesn't! She loves you as dearly as ever mother loved a son! I only said that because you put me in such a God-damned rage, raking up the past, and saying you hate me—

EDMUND

Dully.

I didn't mean it, Papa.

He suddenly smiles—kidding a bit drunkenly.

I'm like Mama, I can't help liking you, in spite of everything.

TYRONE
Grins a bit drunkenly in return.

I might say the same of you. You're no great shakes as a son. It's a case of "A poor thing but mine own."

They both chuckle with real, if alcoholic, affection. Tyrone changes the subject.

What's happened to our game? Whose play is it?

EDMUND

Yours, I guess.

Tyrone plays a card which Edmund takes and the game gets forgotten again.

TYRONE

You mustn't let yourself be too downhearted, lad, by the bad news you had today. Both the doctors promised me, if you obey orders at this place you're going, you'll be cured in six months, or a year at most.

EDMUND
His face hard again.

Don't kid me. You don't believe that.

TYRONE
Too vehemently.

Of course I believe it! Why shouldn't I believe it when both Hardy and the specialist— ?

EDMUND

You think I'm going to die.

TYRONE

That's a lie! You're crazy!

EDMUND
More bitterly.

So why waste money? That's why you're sending me to a state farm—

TYRONE
In guilty confusion.

What state farm? It's the Hilltown Sanatorium, that's all I know, and both doctors said it was the best place for you.

143

EDMUND

Scathingly.

For the money! That is, for nothing, or practically nothing. Don't lie, Papa! You know damned well Hilltown Sanatorium is a state institution! Jamie suspected you'd cry poorhouse to Hardy and he wormed the truth out of him.

TYRONE

Furiously.

That drunken loafer! I'll kick him out in the gutter! He's poisoned your mind against me ever since you were old enough to listen!

EDMUND

You can't deny it's the truth about the state farm, can you?

TYRONE

It's not true the way you look at it! What if it is run by the state? That's nothing against it. The state has the money to make a better place than any private sanatorium. And why shouldn't I take advantage of it? It's my right—and yours. We're residents. I'm a property owner. I help to support it. I'm taxed to death—

EDMUND

With bitter irony.

Yes, on property valued at a quarter of a million.

TYRONE

Lies! It's all mortgaged!

EDMUND

Hardy and the specialist know what you're worth. I wonder what they thought of you when they heard you moaning poorhouse and showing you wanted to wish me on charity!

TYRONE

It's a lie! All I told them was I couldn't afford any millionaire's sanatorium because I was land poor. That's the truth!

EDMUND

And then you went to the Club to meet McGuire and let him stick you with another bum piece of property!

As Tyrone starts to deny.

144

Don't lie about it! We met McGuire in the hotel bar after he left you. Jamie kidded him about hooking you, and he winked and laughed!

TYRONE
Lying feebly.
He's a liar if he said—

EDMUND
Don't lie about it!
With gathering intensity.
God, Papa, ever since I went to sea and was on my own, and found out what hard work for little pay was, and what it felt like to be broke, and starve, and camp on park benches because I had no place to sleep, I've tried to be fair to you because I knew what you'd been up against as a kid. I've tried to make allowances. Christ, you have to make allowances in this damned family or go nuts! I have tried to make allowances for myself when I remember all the rotten stuff I've pulled! I've tried to feel like Mama that you can't help being what you are where money is concerned. But God Almighty, this last stunt of yours is too much! It makes me want to puke! Not because of the rotten way you're treating me. To hell with that! I've treated you rottenly, in my way, more than once. But to think when it's a question of your son having consumption, you can show yourself up before the whole town as such a stinking old tightwad! Don't you know Hardy will talk and the whole damned town will know! Jesus, Papa, haven't you any pride or shame?

Bursting with rage.
And don't think I'll let you get away with it! I won't go to any damned state farm just to save you a few lousy dollars to buy more bum property with! You stinking old miser— !
He chokes huskily, his voice trembling with rage, and then is shaken by a fit of coughing.

TYRONE
Has shrunk back in his chair under this attack, his guilty contrition greater than his anger. He stammers.
Be quiet! Don't say that to me! You're drunk! I won't mind you. Stop coughing, lad. You've got yourself worked up over nothing.

Who said you had to go to this Hilltown place? You can go anywhere you like. I don't give a damn what it costs. All I care about is to have you get well. Don't call me a stinking miser, just because I don't want doctors to think I'm a millionaire they can swindle.

> *Edmund has stopped coughing. He looks sick and weak. His father stares at him frightenedly.*

You look weak, lad. You'd better take a bracer.

EDMUND

> *Grabs the bottle and pours his glass brimfull—weakly.*

Thanks.

> *He gulps down the whiskey.*

TYRONE

> *Pours himself a big drink, which empties the bottle, and drinks it. His head bows and he stares dully at the cards on the table—vaguely.*

Whose play is it?

> *He goes on dully, without resentment.*

A stinking old miser. Well, maybe you're right. Maybe I can't help being, although all my life since I had anything I've thrown money over the bar to buy drinks for everyone in the house, or loaned money to sponges I knew would never pay it back—

> *With a loose-mouthed sneer of self-contempt.*

But, of course, that was in barrooms, when I was full of whiskey. I can't feel that way about it when I'm sober in my home. It was at home I first learned the value of a dollar and the fear of the poorhouse. I've never been able to believe in my luck since. I've always feared it would change and everything I had would be taken away. But still, the more property you own, the safer you think you are. That may not be logical, but it's the way I have to feel. Banks fail, and your money's gone, but you think you can keep land beneath your feet.

> *Abruptly his tone becomes scornfully superior.*

You said you realized what I'd been up against as a boy. The hell you do! How could you? You've had everything—nurses, schools, college, though you didn't stay there. You've had food, clothing. Oh, I know you had a fling of hard work with your back and hands, a bit of being homeless and penniless in a foreign land, and I respect

146

you for it. But it was a game of romance and adventure to you. It was play.

EDMUND
Dully sarcastic.
Yes, particularly the time I tried to commit suicide at Jimmie the Priest's, and almost did.

TYRONE
You weren't in your right mind. No son of mine would ever— You were drunk.

EDMUND
I was stone cold sober. That was the trouble. I'd stopped to think too long.

TYRONE
With drunken peevishness.
Don't start your damned atheist morbidness again! I don't care to listen. I was trying to make plain to you—
Scornfully.
What do you know of the value of a dollar? When I was ten my father deserted my mother and went back to Ireland to die. Which he did soon enough, and deserved to, and I hope he's roasting in hell. He mistook rat poison for flour, or sugar, or something. There was gossip it wasn't by mistake but that's a lie. No one in my family ever—

EDMUND
My bet is, it wasn't by mistake.

TYRONE
More morbidness! Your brother put that in your head. The worst he can suspect is the only truth for him. But never mind. My mother was left, a stranger in a strange land, with four small children, me and a sister a little older and two younger than me. My two older brothers had moved to other parts. They couldn't help. They were hard put to it to keep themselves alive. There was no damned romance in our poverty. Twice we were evicted from the miserable hovel we called home, with my mother's few sticks of furniture thrown out in the street, and my mother and sisters crying. I cried,

147

too, though I tried hard not to, because I was the man of the family. At ten years old! There was no more school for me. I worked twelve hours a day in a machine shop, learning to make files. A dirty barn of a place where rain dripped through the roof, where you roasted in summer, and there was no stove in winter, and your hands got numb with cold, where the only light came through two small filthy windows, so on grey days I'd have to sit bent over with my eyes almost touching the files in order to see! You talk of work! And what do you think I got for it? Fifty cents a week! It's the truth! Fifty cents a week! And my poor mother washed and scrubbed for the Yanks by the day, and my older sister sewed, and my two younger stayed at home to keep the house. We never had clothes enough to wear, nor enough food to eat. Well I remember one Thanksgiving, or maybe it was Christmas, when some Yank in whose house mother had been scrubbing gave her a dollar extra for a present, and on the way home she spent it all on food. I can remember her hugging and kissing us and saying with tears of joy running down her tired face: "Glory be to God, for once in our lives we'll have enough for each of us!"

He wipes tears from his eyes.

A fine, brave, sweet woman. There never was a braver or finer.

EDMUND
Moved.
Yes, she must have been.

TYRONE
Her one fear was she'd get old and sick and have to die in the poorhouse.

He pauses—then adds with grim humor.

It was in those days I learned to be a miser. A dollar was worth so much then. And once you've learned a lesson, it's hard to unlearn it. You have to look for bargains. If I took this state farm sanatorium for a good bargain, you'll have to forgive me. The doctors did tell me it's a good place. You must believe that, Edmund. And I swear I never meant you to go there if you didn't want to.

Vehemently.

You can choose any place you like! Never mind what it costs! Any place I can afford. Any place you like—within reason.

148

At this qualification, a grin twitches Edmund's lips. His resentment has gone. His father goes on with an elaborately offhand, casual air.

There was another sanatorium the specialist recommended. He said it had a record as good as any place in the country. It's endowed by a group of millionaire factory owners, for the benefit of their workers principally, but you're eligible to go there because you're a resident. There's such a pile of money behind it, they don't have to charge much. It's only seven dollars a week but you get ten times that value.

Hastily.

I don't want to persuade you to anything, understand. I'm simply repeating what I was told.

EDMUND

Concealing his smile—casually.

Oh, I know that. It sounds like a good bargain to me. I'd like to go there. So that settles that.

Abruptly he is miserably desperate again—dully.

It doesn't matter a damn now, anyway. Let's forget it!

Changing the subject.

How about our game? Whose play is it?

TYRONE

Mechanically.

I don't know. Mine, I guess. No, it's yours.

Edmund plays a card. His father takes it. Then about to play from his hand, he again forgets the game.

Yes, maybe life overdid the lesson for me, and made a dollar worth too much, and the time came when that mistake ruined my career as a fine actor.

Sadly.

I've never admitted this to anyone before, lad, but tonight I'm so heartsick I feel at the end of everything, and what's the use of fake pride and pretense. That God-damned play I bought for a song and made such a great success in—a great money success—it ruined me with its promise of an easy fortune. I didn't want to do anything else, and by the time I woke up to the fact I'd become a slave to the damned thing and did try other plays, it was too late. They had identified me with that one part, and didn't want me in anything else. They were right, too. I'd lost the great talent I once had through years of easy repetition, never learning a new part, never really working hard. Thirty-five to forty thousand dollars net profit a season like snapping your fingers! It was too great a temptation. Yet before I bought the damned thing I was considered one of the three or four young actors with the greatest artistic promise in America. I'd worked like hell. I'd left a good job as a machinist to take supers' parts because I loved the theater. I was wild with ambition. I read all the plays ever written. I studied Shakespeare as you'd study the Bible. I educated myself. I got rid of an Irish brogue you could cut with a knife. I loved Shakespeare. I would have acted in any of his plays for nothing, for the joy of being alive in his great poetry. And I acted well in him. I felt inspired by him. I could have been a great Shakespearean actor, if I'd kept on. I know that! In 1874 when Edwin Booth came to the theater in Chicago where I was leading man, I played Cassius to his Brutus one night, Brutus to his Cassius the next, Othello to his Iago, and so on. The first night I played Othello, he said to our manager, "That young man is playing Othello better than I ever did!"

> *Proudly.*

That from Booth, the greatest actor of his day or any other! And it was true! And I was only twenty-seven years old! As I look back on it now, that night was the high spot in my career. I had life where I wanted it! And for a time after that I kept on upward with ambition high. Married your mother. Ask her what I was like in those days. Her love was an added incentive to ambition. But a few years later my good bad luck made me find the big money-maker. It wasn't that in my eyes at first. It was a great romantic part I knew I could play better than anyone. But it was a great box office success from the start—and then life had me where it wanted me—at from thirty-five to forty thousand net profit a season! A fortune in those days—or even in these.

> *Bitterly.*

What the hell was it I wanted to buy, I wonder, that was worth—Well, no matter. It's a late day for regrets.

> *He glances vaguely at his cards.*

My play, isn't it?

EDMUND
Moved, stares at his father with understanding—slowly.
I'm glad you've told me this, Papa. I know you a lot better now.

TYRONE
With a loose, twisted smile.
Maybe I shouldn't have told you. Maybe you'll only feel more contempt for me. And it's a poor way to convince you of the value of a dollar.
Then as if this phrase automatically aroused an habitual association in his mind, he glances up at the chandelier disapprovingly.
The glare from those extra lights hurts my eyes. You don't mind if I turn them out, do you? We don't need them, and there's no use making the Electric Company rich.

EDMUND
Controlling a wild impulse to laugh—agreeably.
No, sure not. Turn them out.

TYRONE
Gets heavily and a bit waveringly to his feet and gropes uncertainly for the lights—his mind going back to its line of thought.
No, I don't know what the hell it was I wanted to buy.
He clicks out one bulb.
On my solemn oath, Edmund, I'd gladly face not having an acre of land to call my own, nor a penny in the bank—
He clicks out another bulb.
I'd be willing to have no home but the poorhouse in my old age if I could look back now on having been the fine artist I might have been.
He turns out the third bulb, so only the reading lamp is on, and sits down again heavily. Edmund suddenly cannot hold back a burst of strained, ironical laughter. Tyrone is hurt.
What the devil are you laughing at?

EDMUND
Not at you, Papa. At life. It's so damned crazy.

TYRONE
Growls.

More of your morbidness! There's nothing wrong with life. It's we
who—

He quotes.

"The fault, dear Brutus, is not in our stars, but in ourselves that we
are underlings."

He pauses—then sadly.

The praise Edwin Booth gave my Othello. I made the manager put
down his exact words in writing. I kept it in my wallet for years. I
used to read it every once in a while until finally it made me feel so
bad I didn't want to face it any more. Where is it now, I wonder?
Somewhere in this house. I remember I put it away carefully—

EDMUND

With a wry ironical sadness.

It might be in an old trunk in the attic, along with Mama's wedding
dress.

Then as his father stares at him, he adds quickly.

For Pete's sake, if we're going to play cards, let's play.

*He takes the card his father had played and leads. For a
moment, they play the game, like mechanical chess players.
Then Tyrone stops, listening to a sound upstairs.*

TYRONE

She's still moving around. God knows when she'll go to sleep.

EDMUND

Pleads tensely.

For Christ's sake, Papa, forget it!

*He reaches out and pours a drink. Tyrone starts to protest,
then gives it up. Edmund drinks. He puts down the glass.
His expression changes. When he speaks it is as if he were
deliberately giving way to drunkenness and seeking to hide
behind a maudlin manner.*

Yes, she moves above and beyond us, a ghost haunting the past, and
here we sit pretending to forget, but straining our ears listening for
the slightest sound, hearing the fog drip from the eaves like the un-
even tick of a rundown, crazy clock—or like the dreary tears of a
trollop spattering in a puddle of stale beer on a honky-tonk table top!

He laughs with maudlin appreciation.

Not so bad, that last, eh? Original, not Baudelaire. Give me credit!
Then with alcoholic talkativeness.
You've just told me some high spots in your memories. Want
to hear mine? They're all connected with the sea. Here's one. When
I was on the Squarehead square rigger, bound for Buenos Aires.
Full moon in the Trades. The old hooker driving fourteen knots. I
lay on the bowsprit, facing astern, with the water foaming into spume
under me, the masts with every sail white in the moonlight, towering
high above me. I became drunk with the beauty and singing rhythm
of it, and for a moment I lost myself—actually lost my life. I was
set free! I dissolved in the sea, became white sails and flying spray,
became beauty and rhythm, became moonlight and the ship and the
high dim-starred sky! I belonged, without past or future, within
peace and unity and a wild joy, within something greater than my
own life, or the life of Man, to Life itself! To God, if you want to
put it that way. Then another time, on the American Line, when I
was lookout on the crow's nest in the dawn watch. A calm sea, that
time. Only a lazy ground swell and a slow drowsy roll of the ship.
The passengers asleep and none of the crew in sight. No sound of
man. Black smoke pouring from the funnels behind and beneath me.
Dreaming, not keeping lookout, feeling alone, and above, and apart,
watching the dawn creep like a painted dream over the sky and sea
which slept together. Then the moment of ecstatic freedom came.
The peace, the end of the quest, the last harbor, the joy of belonging
to a fulfillment beyond men's lousy, pitiful, greedy fears and hopes
and dreams! And several other times in my life, when I was swim-
ming far out, or lying alone on a beach, I have had the same experience. Became the sun, the hot sand, green seaweed anchored to a
rock, swaying in the tide. Like a saint's vision of beatitude. Like the
veil of things as they seem drawn back by an unseen hand. For a
second you see—and seeing the secret, are the secret. For a second
there is meaning! Then the hand lets the veil fall and you are alone,
lost in the fog again, and you stumble on toward nowhere, for no
good reason!
He grins wryly.
It was a great mistake, my being born a man, I would have been
much more successful as a sea gull or a fish. As it is, I will always be
a stranger who never feels at home, who does not really want and

is not really wanted, who can never belong, who must always be a little in love with death!

TYRONE
Stares at him—impressed.
Yes, there's the makings of a poet in you all right.
Then protesting uneasily.
But that's morbid craziness about not being wanted and loving death.

EDMUND
Sardonically.
The *makings* of a poet. No, I'm afraid I'm like the guy who is always panhandling for a smoke. He hasn't even got the makings. He's got only the habit. I couldn't touch what I tried to tell you just now. I just stammered. That's the best I'll ever do, I mean, if I live. Well, it will be faithful realism, at least. Stammering is the native eloquence of us fog people.
A pause. Then they both jump startledly as there is a noise from outside the house, as if someone had stumbled and fallen on the front steps. Edmund grins.
Well, that sounds like the absent brother. He must have a peach of a bun on.

TYRONE
Scowling.
That loafer! He caught the last car, bad luck to it.
He gets to his feet.
Get him to bed, Edmund. I'll go out on the porch. He has a tongue like an adder when he's drunk. I'd only lose my temper.
He goes out the door to the side porch as the front door in the hall bangs shut behind Jamie. Edmund watches with amusement Jamie's wavering progress through the front parlor. Jamie comes in. He is very drunk and woozy on his legs. His eyes are glassy, his face bloated, his speech blurred, his mouth slack like his father's, a leer on his lips.

JAMIE
Swaying and blinking in the doorway—in a loud voice.
What ho! What ho!

EDMUND
Sharply.
Nix on the loud noise!

JAMIE
Blinks at him.
Oh, hello, Kid.
With great seriousness.
I'm as drunk as a fiddler's bitch.

EDMUND
Dryly.
Thanks for telling me your great secret.

JAMIE
Grins foolishly.
Yes. Unneshesary information Number One, eh?
He bends and slaps at the knees of his trousers.
Had serious accident. The fron steps tried to trample on me. Took
advantage of fog to waylay me. Ought to be a lighthouse out there.
Dark in here, too.
Scowling.
What the hell is this, the morgue? Lesh have some light on sibject.
He sways forward to the table, reciting Kipling.
"Ford, ford, ford o' Kabul river,
 Ford o' Kabul river in the dark!
 Keep the crossing-stakes beside you, an' they will surely guide you
 'Cross the ford o' Kabul river in the dark."
*He fumbles at the chandelier and manages to turn on the
three bulbs.*
Thash more like it. To hell with old Gaspard. Where is the old
tightwad?

EDMUND
Out on the porch.

JAMIE
Can't expect us to live in the Black Hole of Calcutta.
His eyes fix on the full bottle of whiskey.
Say! Have I got the d.t.'s?
He reaches out fumblingly and grabs it.

By God, it's real. What's matter with the Old Man tonight? Must be ossified to forget he left this out. Grab opportunity by the forelock. Key to my success.

> *He slops a big drink into a glass.*

EDMUND

You're stinking now. That will knock you stiff.

JAMIE

Wisdom from the mouth of babes. Can the wise stuff, Kid. You're still wet behind the ears.

> *He lowers himself into a chair, holding the drink carefully aloft.*

EDMUND

All right. Pass out if you want to.

JAMIE

Can't, that's trouble. Had enough to sink a ship, but can't sink. Well, here's hoping.

> *He drinks.*

EDMUND

Shove over the bottle. I'll have one, too.

JAMIE

> *With sudden, big-brotherly solicitude, grabbing the bottle.*

No, you don't. Not while I'm around. Remember doctor's orders. Maybe no one else gives a damn if you die, but I do. My kid brother. I love your guts, Kid. Everything else is gone. You're all I've got left.

> *Pulling bottle closer to him.*

So no booze for you, if I can help it.

> *Beneath his drunken sentimentality there is a genuine sincerity.*

EDMUND

> *Irritably.*

Oh, lay off it.

JAMIE

> *Is hurt and his face hardens.*

You don't believe I care, eh? Just drunken bull.

> *He shoves the bottle over.*

All right. Go ahead and kill yourself.

EDMUND

> *Seeing he is hurt—affectionately.*

Sure I know you care, Jamie, and I'm going on the wagon. But tonight doesn't count. Too many damned things have happened today.

> *He pours a drink.*

Here's how.

> *He drinks.*

JAMIE

> *Sobers up momentarily and with a pitying look.*

I know, Kid. It's been a lousy day for you.

> *Then with sneering cynicism.*

I'll bet old Gaspard hasn't tried to keep you off booze. Probably give you a case to take with you to the state farm for pauper patients. The sooner you kick the bucket, the less expense.

> *With contemptuous hatred.*

What a bastard to have for a father! Christ, if you put him in a book, no one would believe it!

EDMUND

> *Defensively.*

Oh, Papa's all right, if you try to understand him—and keep your sense of humor.

JAMIE

> *Cynically.*

He's been putting on the old sob act for you, eh? He can always kid you. But not me. Never again.

> *Then slowly.*

Although, in a way, I do feel sorry for him about one thing. But he has even that coming to him. He's to blame.

> *Hurriedly.*

But to hell with that.

> *He grabs the bottle and pours another drink, appearing very drunk again.*

That lash drink's getting me. This one ought to put the lights out. Did you tell Gaspard I got it out of Doc Hardy this sanatorium is a charity dump?

EDMUND
Reluctantly.
Yes. I told him I wouldn't go there. It's all settled now. He said I can go anywhere I want.
He adds, smiling without resentment.
Within reason, of course.

JAMIE
Drunkenly imitating his father.
Of course, lad. Anything within reason.
Sneering.
That means another cheap dump. Old Gaspard, the miser in "The Bells," that's a part he can play without make-up.

EDMUND
Irritably.
Oh, shut up, will you. I've heard that Gaspard stuff a million times.

JAMIE
Shrugs his shoulders—thickly.
Aw right, if you're shatisfied—let him get away with it. It's your funeral—I mean, I hope it won't be.

EDMUND
Changing the subject.
What did you do uptown tonight? Go to Mamie Burns?

JAMIE
Very drunk, his head nodding.
Sure thing. Where else could I find suitable feminine companionship? And love. Don't forget love. What is a man without a good woman's love? A God-damned hollow shell.

EDMUND
Chuckles tipsily, letting himself go now and be drunk.
You're a nut.

JAMIE

Quotes with gusto from Oscar Wilde's "The Harlot's House."

"Then, turning to my love, I said,
'The dead are dancing with the dead,
The dust is whirling with the dust.'

But she—she heard the violin,
And left my side and entered in:
Love passed into the house of lust.

Then suddenly the tune went false,
The dancers wearied of the waltz . . ."

He breaks off, thickly.

Not strictly accurate. If my love was with me, I didn't notice it. She must have been a ghost.

He pauses.

Guess which one of Mamie's charmers I picked to bless me with her woman's love. It'll hand you a laugh, Kid. I picked Fat Violet.

EDMUND

Laughs drunkenly.

No, honest? Some pick! God, she weighs a ton. What the hell for, a joke?

JAMIE

No joke. Very serious. By the time I hit Mamie's dump I felt very sad about myself and all the other poor bums in the world. Ready for a weep on any old womanly bosom. You know how you get when John Barleycorn turns on the soft music inside you. Then, soon as I got in the door, Mamie began telling me all her troubles. Beefed how rotten business was, and she was going to give Fat Violet the gate. Customers didn't fall for Vi. Only reason she'd kept her was she could play the piano. Lately Vi's gone on drunks and been too boiled to play, and was eating her out of house and home, and although Vi was a goodhearted dumbbell, and she felt sorry for her because she didn't know how the hell she'd make a living, still business was business, and she couldn't afford to run a home for fat tarts. Well, that made me feel sorry for Fat Violet, so I squandered two bucks of your dough to escort her upstairs. With no dishonorable intentions whatever. I like them fat, but not that fat. All I wanted was a little heart-to-heart talk concerning the infinite sorrow of life.

EDMUND
Chuckles drunkenly.
Poor Vi! I'll bet you recited Kipling and Swinburne and Dowson and gave her "I have been faithful to thee, Cynara, in my fashion."

JAMIE
Grins loosely.
Sure—with the Old Master, John Barleycorn, playing soft music. She stood it for a while. Then she got good and sore. Got the idea I took her upstairs for a joke. Gave me a grand bawling out. Said she was better than a drunken bum who recited poetry. Then she began to cry. So I had to say I loved her because she was fat, and she wanted to believe that, and I stayed with her to prove it, and that cheered her up, and she kissed me when I left, and said she'd fallen hard for me, and we both cried a little more in the hallway, and everything was fine, except Mamie Burns thought I'd gone bughouse.

EDMUND
Quotes derisively.

> "Harlots and
> Hunted have pleasures of their own to give,
> The vulgar herd can never understand."

JAMIE
Nods his head drunkenly.
Egzactly! Hell of a good time, at that. You should have stuck around with me, Kid. Mamie Burns inquired after you. Sorry to hear you were sick. She meant it, too.
He pauses—then with maudlin humor, in a ham-actor tone.
This night has opened my eyes to a great career in store for me, my boy! I shall give the art of acting back to the performing seals, which are its most perfect expression. By applying my natural God-given talents in their proper sphere, I shall attain the pinnacle of success! I'll be the lover of the fat woman in Barnum and Bailey's circus!
Edmund laughs. Jamie's mood changes to arrogant disdain.
Pah! Imagine me sunk to the fat girl in a hick town hooker shop!

Me! Who have made some of the best-lookers on Broadway sit up and beg!

> *He quotes from Kipling's "Sestina of the Tramp-Royal."*
> "Speakin' in general, I 'ave tried 'em all,
> The 'appy roads that take you o'er the world."
> *With sodden melancholy.*

Not so apt. Happy roads is bunk. Weary roads is right. Get you nowhere fast. That's where I've got—nowhere. Where everyone lands in the end, even if most of the suckers won't admit it.

> EDMUND
> *Derisively.*

Can it! You'll be crying in a minute.

> JAMIE
> *Starts and stares at his brother for a second with bitter hostility—thickly.*

Don't get—too damned fresh.

> *Then abruptly.*

But you're right. To hell with repining! Fat Violet's a good kid. Glad I stayed with her. Christian act. Cured her blues. Hell of a good time. You should have stuck with me, Kid. Taken your mind off your troubles. What's the use coming home to get the blues over what can't be helped. All over—finished now—not a hope!

> *He stops, his head nodding drunkenly, his eyes closing— then suddenly he looks up, his face hard, and quotes jeeringly.*
> "If I were hanged on the highest hill,
> Mother o' mine, O mother o' mine!
> I know whose love would follow me still . . . "

> EDMUND
> *Violently.*

Shut up!

> JAMIE
> *In a cruel, sneering tone with hatred in it.*

Where's the hophead? Gone to sleep?

> *Edmund jerks as if he'd been struck. There is a tense silence.*

Edmund's face looks stricken and sick. Then in a burst of rage he springs from his chair.

EDMUND

You dirty bastard!

He punches his brother in the face, a blow that glances off the cheekbone. For a second Jamie reacts pugnaciously and half rises from his chair to do battle, but suddenly he seems to sober up to a shocked realization of what he has said and he sinks back limply.

JAMIE
Miserably.

Thanks, Kid. I certainly had that coming. Don't know what made me—booze talking— You know me, Kid.

EDMUND
His anger ebbing.

I know you'd never say that unless— But God, Jamie, no matter how drunk you are, it's no excuse!
He pauses—miserably.
I'm sorry I hit you. You and I never scrap—that bad.
He sinks back on his chair.

JAMIE
Huskily.

It's all right. Glad you did. My dirty tongue. Like to cut it out.
He hides his face in his hands—dully.
I suppose it's because I feel so damned sunk. Because this time Mama had me fooled. I really believed she had it licked. She thinks I always believe the worst, but this time I believed the best.
His voice flutters.
I suppose I can't forgive her—yet. It meant so much. I'd begun to hope, if she'd beaten the game, I could, too.
He begins to sob, and the horrible part of his weeping is that it appears sober, not the maudlin tears of drunkenness.

EDMUND
Blinking back tears himself.

God, don't I know how you feel! Stop it, Jamie!

JAMIE
> *Trying to control his sobs.*

I've known about Mama so much longer than you. Never forget the first time I got wise. Caught her in the act with a hypo. Christ, I'd never dreamed before that any women but whores took dope!

> *He pauses.*

And then this stuff of you getting consumption. It's got me licked. We've been more than brothers. You're the only pal I've ever had. I love your guts. I'd do anything for you.

EDMUND
> *Reaches out and pats his arm.*

I know that, Jamie.

JAMIE
> *His crying over—drops his hands from his face—with a strange bitterness.*

Yet I'll bet you've heard Mama and old Gaspard spill so much bunk about my hoping for the worst, you suspect right now I'm thinking to myself that Papa is old and can't last much longer, and if you were to die, Mama and I would get all he's got, and so I'm probably hoping—

EDMUND
> *Indignantly.*

Shut up, you damned fool! What the hell put that in your nut?

> *He stares at his brother accusingly.*

Yes, that's what I'd like to know. What put that in your mind?

JAMIE
> *Confusedly—appearing drunk again.*

Don't be a dumbbell! What I said! Always suspected of hoping for the worst. I've got so I can't help—

> *Then drunkenly resentful.*

What are you trying to do, accuse me? Don't play the wise guy with me! I've learned more of life than you'll ever know! Just because you've read a lot of highbrow junk, don't think you can fool me! You're only an overgrown kid! Mama's baby and Papa's pet! The family White Hope! You've been getting a swelled head lately. About nothing! About a few poems in a hick town newspaper!

Hell, I used to write better stuff for the Lit magazine in college! You better wake up! You're setting no rivers on fire! You let hick town boobs flatter you with bunk about your future—

> *Abruptly his tone changes to disgusted contrition. Edmund has looked away from him, trying to ignore this tirade.*

Hell, Kid, forget it. That goes for Sweeny. You know I don't mean it. No one is prouder you've started to make good.

> *Drunkenly assertive.*

Why shouldn't I be proud? Hell, it's purely selfish. You reflect credit on me. I've had more to do with bringing you up than anyone. I wised you up about women, so you'd never be a fall guy, or make any mistakes you didn't want to make! And who steered you on to reading poetry first? Swinburne, for example? I did! And because I once wanted to write, I planted it in your mind that someday you'd write! Hell, you're more than my brother. I made you! You're my Frankenstein!

> *He has risen to a note of drunken arrogance. Edmund is grinning with amusement now.*

EDMUND

All right, I'm your Frankenstein. So let's have a drink.

> *He laughs.*

You crazy nut!

JAMIE
> *Thickly.*

I'll have a drink. Not you. Got to take care of you.

> *He reaches out with a foolish grin of doting affection and grabs his brother's hand.*

Don't be scared of this sanatorium business. Hell, you can beat that standing on your head. Six months and you'll be in the pink. Probably haven't got consumption at all. Doctors lot of fakers. Told me years ago to cut out booze or I'd soon be dead—and here I am. They're all con men. Anything to grab your dough. I'll bet this state farm stuff is political graft game. Doctors get a cut for every patient they send.

EDMUND
> *Disgustedly amused.*

You're the limit! At the Last Judgment, you'll be around telling everyone it's in the bag.

> JAMIE

And I'll be right. Slip a piece of change to the Judge and be saved, but if you're broke you can go to hell!

> *He grins at this blasphemy and Edmund has to laugh. Jamie goes on.*

"Therefore put money in thy purse." That's the only dope.

> *Mockingly.*

The secret of my success! Look what it's got me!

> *He lets Edmund's hand go to pour a big drink, and gulps it down. He stares at his brother with bleary affection—takes his hand again and begins to talk thickly but with a strange, convincing sincerity.*

Listen, Kid, you'll be going away. May not get another chance to talk. Or might not be drunk enough to tell you truth. So got to tell you now. Something I ought to have told you long ago—for your own good.

> *He pauses—struggling with himself. Edmund stares, impressed and uneasy. Jamie blurts out.*

Not drunken bull, but "in vino veritas" stuff. You better take it seriously. Want to warn you—against me. Mama and Papa are right. I've been rotten bad influence. And worst of it is, I did it on purpose.

> EDMUND
> *Uneasily.*

Shut up! I don't want to hear—

> JAMIE

Nix, Kid! You listen! Did it on purpose to make a bum of you. Or part of me did. A big part. That part that's been dead so long. That hates life. My putting you wise so you'd learn from my mistakes. Believed that myself at times, but it's a fake. Made my mistakes look good. Made getting drunk romantic. Made whores fascinating vampires instead of poor, stupid, diseased slobs they really are. Made fun of work as sucker's game. Never wanted you succeed and make me look even worse by comparison. Wanted you to fail. Always jealous of you. Mama's baby, Papa's pet!

He stares at Edmund with increasing enmity.

And it was your being born that started Mama on dope. I know that's not your fault, but all the same, God damn you, I can't help hating your guts— !

EDMUND
Almost frightenedly.
Jamie! Cut it out! You're crazy!

JAMIE
But don't get wrong idea, Kid. I love you more than I hate you. My saying what I'm telling you now proves it. I run the risk you'll hate me—and you're all I've got left. But I didn't mean to tell you that last stuff—go that far back. Don't know what made me. What I wanted to say is, I'd like to see you become the greatest success in the world. But you'd better be on your guard. Because I'll do my damnedest to make you fail. Can't help it. I hate myself. Got to take revenge. On everyone else. Especially you. Oscar Wilde's "Reading Gaol" has the dope twisted. The man was dead and so he had to kill the thing he loved. That's what it ought to be. The dead part of me hopes you won't get well. Maybe he's even glad the game has got Mama again! He wants company, he doesn't want to be the only corpse around the house!
He gives a hard, tortured laugh.

EDMUND
Jesus, Jamie! You really have gone crazy!

JAMIE
Think it over and you'll see I'm right. Think it over when you're away from me in the sanatorium. Make up your mind you've got to tie a can to me—get me out of your life—think of me as dead—tell people, "I had a brother, but he's dead." And when you come back, look out for me. I'll be waiting to welcome you with that "my old pal" stuff, and give you the glad hand, and at the first good chance I get stab you in the back.

EDMUND
Shut up! I'll be God-damned if I'll listen to you any more—

JAMIE
As if he hadn't heard.

166

Only don't forget me. Remember I warned you—for your sake.
Give me credit. Greater love hath no man than this, that he saveth
his brother from himself.

> *Very drunkenly, his head bobbing.*

That's all. Feel better now. Gone to confession. Know you absolve
me, don't you, Kid? You understand. You're a damned fine kid.
Ought to be. I made you. So go and get well. Don't die on me.
You're all I've got left. God bless you, Kid.

> *His eyes close. He mumbles.*

That last drink—the old K. O.

> *He falls into a drunken doze, not completely asleep. Ed-
> mund buries his face in his hands miserably. Tyrone comes
> in quietly through the screen door from the porch, his dressing
> gown wet with fog, the collar turned up around his throat.
> His face is stern and disgusted but at the same time pitying.
> Edmund does not notice his entrance.*

TYRONE

> *In a low voice.*

Thank God he's asleep.

> *Edmund looks up with a start.*

I thought he'd never stop talking.

> *He turns down the collar of his dressing gown.*

We'd better let him stay where he is and sleep it off.

> *Edmund remains silent. Tyrone regards him—then goes on.*

I heard the last part of his talk. It's what I've warned you. I hope
you'll heed the warning, now it comes from his own mouth.

> *Edmund gives no sign of having heard.*

> *Tyrone adds pityingly.*

But don't take it too much to heart, lad. He loves to exaggerate the
worst of himself when he's drunk. He's devoted to you. It's the one
good thing left in him.

> *He looks down on Jamie with a bitter sadness.*

A sweet spectacle for me! My first-born, who I hoped would bear
my name in honor and dignity, who showed such brilliant promise!

EDMUND

> *Miserably.*

Keep quiet, can't you, Papa?

TYRONE
Pours a drink.

A waste! A wreck, a drunken hulk, done with and finished!

*He drinks. Jamie has become restless, sensing his father's
presence, struggling up from his stupor. Now he gets his
eyes open to blink up at Tyrone. The latter moves back a
step defensively, his face growing hard.*

JAMIE
*Suddenly points a finger at him and recites with dramatic
emphasis.*

Clarence is come, false, fleeting, perjured Clarence,
That stabbed me in the field by Tewksbury.
Seize on him, Furies, take him into torment."
Then resentfully.

What the hell are you staring at?
He recites sardonically from Rossetti.
"Look in my face. My name is Might-Have-Been;
I am also called No More, Too Late, Farewell."

TYRONE
I'm well aware of that, and God knows I don't want to look at it.

EDMUND
Papa! Quit it!

JAMIE
Derisively.

Got a great idea for you, Papa. Put on revival of "The Bells" this
season. Great part in it you can play without make-up. Old Gaspard,
the miser!
Tyrone turns away, trying to control his temper.

EDMUND
Shut up, Jamie!

JAMIE
Jeeringly.

I claim Edwin Booth never saw the day when he could give as good
a performance as a trained seal. Seals are intelligent and honest. They

don't put up any bluffs about the Art of Acting. They admit they're just hams earning their daily fish.

TYRONE
Stung, turns on him in a rage.

You loafer!

EDMUND

Papa! Do you want to start a row that will bring Mama down? Jamie, go back to sleep! You've shot off your mouth too much already.

Tyrone turns away.

JAMIE
Thickly.

All right, Kid. Not looking for argument. Too damned sleepy.

He closes his eyes, his head nodding. Tyrone comes to the table and sits down, turning his chair so he won't look at Jamie. At once he becomes sleepy, too.

TYRONE
Heavily.

I wish to God she'd go to bed so that I could, too.

Drowsily.

I'm dog tired. I can't stay up all night like I used to. Getting old— old and finished.

With a bone-cracking yawn.

Can't keep my eyes open. I think I'll catch a few winks. Why don't you do the same, Edmund? It'll pass the time until she—

His voice trails off. His eyes close, his chin sags, and he begins to breathe heavily through his mouth. Edmund sits tensely. He hears something and jerks nervously forward in his chair, staring through the front parlor into the hall. He jumps up with a hunted, distracted expression. It seems for a second he is going to hide in the back parlor. Then he sits down again and waits, his eyes averted, his hands gripping the arms of his chair. Suddenly all five bulbs of the chandelier in the front parlor are turned on from a wall switch, and a moment later someone starts playing the piano in there— the opening of one of Chopin's simpler waltzes, done with a forgetful, stiff-fingered groping, as if an awkward school-girl were practicing it for the first time. Tyrone starts to wide-awakeness and sober dread, and Jamie's head jerks back and his eyes open. For a moment they listen frozenly. The playing stops as abruptly as it began, and Mary appears in the doorway. She wears a sky-blue dressing gown over her nightdress, dainty slippers with pompons on her bare feet. Her face is paler than ever. Her eyes look enormous. They glisten like polished black jewels. The uncanny thing is that her face now appears so youthful. Experience seems ironed out of it. It is a marble mask of girlish inno-cence, the mouth caught in a shy smile. Her white hair is braided in two pigtails which hang over her breast. Over one arm, carried neglectfully, trailing on the floor, as if she had forgotten she held it, is an old-fashioned white satin wedding gown, trimmed with duchesse lace. She hesitates in the door-way, glancing round the room, her forehead puckered puzzledly, like someone who has come to a room to get something but has become absent-minded on the way and forgotten what it was. They stare at her. She seems aware of them merely as she is aware of other objects in the room, the furniture, the windows, familiar things she accepts auto-matically as naturally belonging there but which she is too preoccupied to notice.

JAMIE
*Breaks the cracking silence—bitterly,
self-defensively sardonic.*

The Mad Scene. Enter Ophelia!

His father and brother both turn on him fiercely. Edmund is quicker. He slaps Jamie across the mouth with the back of his hand.

TYRONE
His voice trembling with suppressed fury.

Good boy, Edmund. The dirty blackguard! His own mother!

JAMIE
Mumbles guiltily, without resentment.

All right, Kid. Had it coming. But I told you how much I'd hoped—
> *He puts his hands over his face and begins to sob.*

TYRONE

I'll kick you out in the gutter tomorrow, so help me God.
> *But Jamie's sobbing breaks his anger, and he turns and shakes his shoulder, pleading.*

Jamie, for the love of God, stop it!
> *Then Mary speaks, and they freeze into silence again, staring at her. She has paid no attention whatever to the incident. It is simply a part of the familiar atmosphere of the room, a background which does not touch her preoccupation; and she speaks aloud to herself, not to them.*

MARY

I play so badly now. I'm all out of practice. Sister Theresa will give me a dreadful scolding. She'll tell me it isn't fair to my father when he spends so much money for extra lessons. She's quite right, it isn't fair, when he's so good and generous, and so proud of me. I'll practice every day from now on. But something horrible has happened to my hands. The fingers have gotten so stiff—
> *She lifts her hands to examine them with a frightened puzzlement.*

The knuckles are all swollen. They're so ugly. I'll have to go to the Infirmary and show Sister Martha.
> *With a sweet smile of affectionate trust.*

She's old and a little cranky, but I love her just the same, and she has things in her medicine chest that'll cure anything. She'll give me something to rub on my hands, and tell me to pray to the Blessed Virgin, and they'll be well again in no time.
> *She forgets her hands and comes into the room, the wedding gown trailing on the floor. She glances around vaguely, her forehead puckered again.*

Let me see. What did I come here to find? It's terrible, how absent-minded I've become. I'm always dreaming and forgetting.

TYRONE
> *In a stifled voice.*

What's that she's carrying, Edmund?

EDMUND

Dully.

Her wedding gown, I suppose.

TYRONE

Christ!

He gets to his feet and stands directly in her path—in anguish.

Mary! Isn't it bad enough— ?

Controlling himself—gently persuasive.

Here, let me take it, dear. You'll only step on it and tear it and get it dirty dragging it on the floor. Then you'd be sorry afterwards.

She lets him take it, regarding him from somewhere far away within herself, without recognition, without either affection or animosity.

MARY

With the shy politeness of a well-bred young girl toward an elderly gentleman who relieves her of a bundle.

Thank you. You are very kind.

She regards the wedding gown with a puzzled interest.

It's a wedding gown. It's very lovely, isn't it?

A shadow crosses her face and she looks vaguely uneasy.

I remember now. I found it in the attic hidden in a trunk. But I don't know what I wanted it for. I'm going to be a nun—that is, if I can only find—

She looks around the room, her forehead puckered again.

What is it I'm looking for? I know it's something I lost.

She moves back from Tyrone, aware of him now only as some obstacle in her path.

TYRONE

In hopeless appeal.

Mary!

But it cannot penetrate her preoccupation. She doesn't seem to hear him. He gives up helplessly, shrinking into himself, even his defensive drunkenness taken from him, leaving him sick and sober. He sinks back on his chair, holding the wedding gown in his arms with an unconscious clumsy, protective gentleness.

172

JAMIE

Drops his hand from his face, his eyes on the table top. He has suddenly sobered up, too—dully.

It's no good, Papa.

He recites from Swinburne's "A Leave-taking" and does it well, simply but with a bitter sadness.

"Let us rise up and part; she will not know.
Let us go seaward as the great winds go,
Full of blown sand and foam; what help is here?
There is no help, for all these things are so,
And all the world is bitter as a tear.
And how these things are, though ye strove to show,
She would not know."

MARY

Looking around her.

Something I miss terribly. It can't be altogether lost.

She starts to move around in back of Jamie's chair.

JAMIE

Turns to look up into her face—and cannot help appealing pleadingly in his turn.

Mama!

She does not seem to hear. He looks away hopelessly.

Hell! What's the use? It's no good.

He recites from "A Leave-taking" again with increased bitterness.

"Let us go hence, my songs; she will not hear.
Let us go hence together without fear;
Keep silence now, for singing-time is over,
And over all old things and all things dear.
She loves not you nor me as all we love her.
Yea, though we sang as angels in her ear,
She would not hear."

MARY

Looking around her.

Something I need terribly. I remember when I had it I was never lonely nor afraid. I can't have lost it forever, I would die if I thought that. Because then there would be no hope.

173

She moves like a sleepwalker, around the back of Jamie's chair, then forward toward left front, passing behind Edmund.

EDMUND

Turns impulsively and grabs her arm. As he pleads he has the quality of a bewilderedly hurt little boy.

Mama! It isn't a summer cold! I've got consumption!

MARY

For a second he seems to have broken through to her. She trembles and her expression becomes terrified. She calls distractedly, as if giving a command to herself.

No!

And instantly she is far away again. She murmurs gently but impersonally.

You must not try to touch me. You must not try to hold me. It isn't right, when I am hoping to be a nun.

He lets his hand drop from her arm. She moves left to the front end of the sofa beneath the windows and sits down, facing front, her hands folded in her lap, in a demure school-girlish pose.

JAMIE

Gives Edmund a strange look of mingled pity and jealous gloating.

You damned fool. It's no good.

He recites again from the Swinburne poem.

"Let us go hence, go hence; she will not see.
Sing all once more together; surely she,
She too, remembering days and words that were,
Will turn a little toward us, sighing; but we,
We are hence, we are gone, as though we had not been there.
Nay, and though all men seeing had pity on me,
She would not see."

TYRONE

Trying to shake off his hopeless stupor.

Oh, we're fools to pay any attention. It's the damned poison. But I've never known her to drown herself in it as deep as this.

Gruffly.

Pass me that bottle, Jamie. And stop reciting that damned morbid poetry. I won't have it in my house!

> *Jamie pushes the bottle toward him. He pours a drink without disarranging the wedding gown he holds carefully over his other arm and on his lap, and shoves the bottle back. Jamie pours his and passes the bottle to Edmund, who, in turn, pours one. Tyrone lifts his glass and his sons follow suit mechanically, but before they can drink Mary speaks and they slowly lower their drinks to the table, forgetting them.*

MARY

> *Staring dreamily before her. Her face looks extraordinarily youthful and innocent. The shyly eager, trusting smile is on her lips as she talks aloud to herself.*

I had a talk with Mother Elizabeth. She is so sweet and good. A saint on earth. I love her dearly. It may be sinful of me but I love her better than my own mother. Because she always understands, even before you say a word. Her kind blue eyes look right into your heart. You can't keep any secrets from her. You couldn't deceive her, even if you were mean enough to want to.

> *She gives a little rebellious toss of her head*
> *—with girlish pique.*

All the same, I don't think she was so understanding this time. I told her I wanted to be a nun. I explained how sure I was of my vocation, that I had prayed to the Blessed Virgin to make me sure, and to find me worthy. I told Mother I had had a true vision when I was praying in the shrine of Our Lady of Lourdes, on the little island in the lake. I said I knew, as surely as I knew I was kneeling there, that the Blessed Virgin had smiled and blessed me with her consent. But Mother Elizabeth told me I must be more sure than that, even, that I must prove it wasn't simply my imagination. She said, if I was so sure, then I wouldn't mind putting myself to a test by going home after I graduated, and living as other girls lived, going out to parties and dances and enjoying myself; and then if after a year or two I still felt sure, I could come back to see her and we would talk it over again.

She tosses her head—indignantly.

I never dreamed Holy Mother would give me such advice! I was really shocked. I said, of course, I would do anything she suggested, but I knew it was simply a waste of time. After I left her, I felt all mixed up, so I went to the shrine and prayed to the Blessed Virgin and found peace again because I knew she heard my prayer and would always love me and see no harm ever came to me so long as I never lost my faith in her.

> *She pauses and a look of growing uneasiness comes over her face. She passes a hand over her forehead as if brushing cobwebs from her brain—vaguely.*

That was in the winter of senior year. Then in the spring something happened to me. Yes, I remember. I fell in love with James Tyrone and was so happy for a time.

> *She stares before her in a sad dream. Tyrone stirs in his chair. Edmund and Jamie remain motionless.*

CURTAIN

Tao House
September 20, 1940